Albedo

Peter Piller Archive
Materials (G)
Albedo

Introduction

This publication accompanies the exhibition *Belegkontrolle* (Document Control), presenting almost twenty years of photographic work by Peter Piller. It adopts a deliberately unconventional format that does not seek to reproduce the artist's oeuvre through the mere reproduction of his images. Instead, this two-part book provides, in the first part, essays on Piller's most important series and cycles, addressing his archival and photographic works, while the second part examines the notion of the archive as a core aspect of the artist's oeuvre, encompassing various views from the worlds of art and culture, psychoanalysis and philosophy.

The exhibition title *Belegkontrolle* is derived from Piller's part-time job in a Hamburg-based media agency where he worked while he was an art student in the mid-1990s. He was tasked with checking the outcome, form, and placement of advertisements by local businesses and companies. In the course of leafing through the daily newspapers to this end, Piller stumbled upon various photographs which he then started to cut out and set aside, archiving them under categories such as *Auto berühren* (Touching Car), *Noch ist nichts zu sehen (Bauerwartungsflächen)* (Nothing Yet to Be Seen [Future Building Sites]), or *Schießende Mädchen* (Shooting Girls). Over the years, this built up into what became the *Peter Piller Archive* of more than seven thousand images with countless subcategories.

The relationship between word and image is an important criterion in Piller's work. Where others may recognize nothing, the artist, through his constantly concentrated observation, develops a keen sense for the hidden qualities of utilitarian photography. Arranged in groups and coded by titles, the found or donated visual material is transposed by Piller into a new artistic order. Alongside the immovable sequence of images in his artist's books, Piller invents no less stringent groups for the exhibition venue itself. In this respect, the plurality of his approach is not dissimilar to that of his fellow artist Hans-Peter Feldmann, who also uses found and self-photographed everyday images as the basis for his collections.

In his introductory essay, Ludwig Seyfarth describes how Piller brings to light basic motifs and similarities by juxtaposing reproductions and concludes that Piller is not so much a Conceptual artist as, rather, an artist who processes and reveals the concepts of the original material. Maren Lübbke-Tidow comes to a similar conclusion and considers that it is the multipart aspect of Piller's series that constitutes the actual "body" of the work. It is the groups of images that provide an open framework for things that are otherwise only vaguely connected. Dieter Roelstraete and Joerg Bader explore different aspects of the artist's gaze in their essays. Whereas Roelstraete attributes a futile male *Schaulust* to the sexually charged secondhand images, Bader finds that the montage of documentary photos possesses a subjective order which, in the spirit of W. G. Sebald, allows a new view of past wars. Using observations from the routine reporting of a Swiss regional newspaper, Elisabetta Antonelli mirrors Peter Piller's pictorial arrangements against the journalistic treatment of local occasions such as ground-breaking ceremonies and other such recurrent events. Marcus Steinweg undertakes a philosophical examination of the indifference of the seemingly banal and argues that it is desire that creates the tension of thinking. Max Küng, on the other hand, puts forward the view that Piller conjures a "gaze without intention;" he finds in the work of the artist an extension of mere seeing to the point of recognition. The first part closes with a text by Peter Piller himself in which the reader learns of a boyhood passion reemerging in later life. While it may appear to be primarily about the decisive moment, it is actually the footnotes that provide the real insight into Piller's artistic approach, in all its impatience, serendipitous mishaps, and doubts: "the first glance is not to be trusted at all."

The second "archive"-part of the publication opens with an essay by Jörg Heiser, who compares the typology of the archival artist in the twentieth and twenty-first centuries with the positions of Marcel Duchamp, Aby Warburg, and Gerhard Richter, spanning a broad arc that also includes Walid Raad and Aleksandra Domanović. Heiser sees potential for the artistic exploration of assertions and fantasies, surmising that truths can be derived from these "porous" states. Psychoanalyst Ben Kafka notes an ambiguously charged relationship between bureaucracy, boredom, and paranoia in (artistic) archival work, while at the same time acknowledging its revolutionary potential. The publication is rounded off by three essays on the issues of memory, storage, and reproduction. Dietmar Dath invites the archive and the generator (as he refers to its future-oriented counterpart) to participate in a fictitious dialogue about their respective dependencies between conservation and renewal. Sociologist Harald Welzer posits that memory cannot be archival because it modifies what is stored; moreover that everything that is retained in a positive vein is implicitly informed by what has been discarded. Media theorist Geert Lovink compares the technological vitality of the digital network, in all its to-and-fro of sending and receiving, with the analogue constancy and long-term legibility of analogue archives – arriving at the conclusion that the Internet is not an archive.

This publication and the exhibition *Belegkontrolle* have been realized in close collaboration with Joerg Bader, Centre de la photographie Genève, Thomas Niemeyer, Städtische Galerie Nordhorn and Ellen Seifermann, Kunsthalle Nürnberg. We owe a joint debt of gratitude to the gallery Capitain Petzel in Berlin for cooperating in mounting the exhibition. We would also like to thank the authors who have so intelligently anchored the oeuvre of Peter Piller within its historical and contemporary context. Finally, our greatest thanks must go to Peter Piller himself for investing such energy and passion in the project over the course of the past two years.

Thomas Seelig, Fotomuseum Winterthur

What Matters Is the Invisible

Peter Piller's Art of Using Photography

Ludwig Seyfarth

The discussion on art and photography has long centered on the question as to whether a technical medium such as photography could actually be art. Anyone interested in creating artistic photographs was careful to make sure that they clearly had the look of art. Spontaneous snapshots generally do not, and thus the history of artistic photography has been shaped by ingenious processes of manipulating the image or complex setups recalling those of a film set.

The more emphatically a photograph is presented as art, the narrower the margin for the unintentional inevitably becomes, because most artistic photographers are concerned with keeping everything under control and delivering results in which the painstaking care of the artistic hand is evident in every detail. With large-format Cibachrome or Diasec prints now rivaling traditional paintings, many fascinating things fall by the wayside – apart from the allure of perfection – that is, more or less everything that the photographer forgot to consider when taking the picture.

Elements that are unconscious to and unintended by the photographer enter into an image by the fact that photographers do not have to visually create what they convey there. It can always happen that something unnoticed becomes part of the picture, and photographers themselves may go unnoticed as they are taking the picture.

A photographer can be far away from the action and leave no traces behind. The photographer thus also becomes a potential perpetrator, and the motif in the photograph a potential crime scene, as described by Walter Benjamin. However, a photographer can also assume the role of a witness, sometimes by chance, when something comes into the image while the photographer is aiming for something completely different. A photographer can control a great deal, but not everything.

Nothing Yet to Be Seen

Peter Piller's interest in the rich imagery to be found far off the beaten track of "artistic photography" was first cultivated when, as a student, he took a job at a Hamburg media agency in 1997, where he spent years working on the evaluation, monitoring, and archiving of local newspapers. In additional to his official duties, he soon began to examine the photographs published in the newspapers that landed on his desk on a daily basis, and he began to cut not only the articles and advertisements required for the company archive out of the newspapers but also many other photographs.

He collected these images and began to assemble them into series. The criteria that he applied to this process would be considered counterproductive to the usual intentions of photographers and image editors. The categories of the archive, also available on the Internet under www.peterpiller.de, almost suggest a surrealist encyclopedia: *Durchschnittene Einweihungsbänder* (Cut Ceremonial Ribbons), *Rätselgewinner präsentieren Geldscheine* (Contest Winners Presenting Banknotes), *Auto berühren* (Touching Car), *Müll als Skulptur* (Garbage as Sculpture). A pile of trash is usually not represented in a regional paper for its sculptural qualities but as a *Stein des Anstosses* (Bone of Contention). This latter rubric encompasses images grouped by their captions and not by their motifs, which leads to very surprising juxtapositions.

The first publication from this archive of photographs from local newspapers was published in 1998 by the publisher Materialverlag at the University of Fine Arts of Hamburg. Entitled *Noch ist nichts zu sehen* (Nothing Yet to Be Seen), this collection of 53 photographs shows various nondescript plots of what seems to be fallow land. Why these sites were photographed in the first place only becomes evident upon reading the captions: "Where cows still graze a new Aldi supermarket will open soon" and "There is nothing yet to be seen, but the City neighborhood park should and must be completed by 1999, the year of the IBA exhibition."

What the photographs portray are lots slated for development, or so-called *Bauerwartungsflächen* (Future Building Sites) in German real-estate jargon. Although on the site one sees nothing of the things to come, the images reveal a good deal. The photograph of the "investment ruin" in the residential neighborhood of Am Steige cleverly plays with scale; in the foreground a sewer protruding out of the landscape seems monumental, dominating over a three-story building in the background. The cement components lying around at Heimannshof give less of an impression of a residential development area, where young families are to be able to build affordably, than of another *bone of contention* – a sculpture in public space that does not at all correspond to the taste of many residents and poses a potential hazard to playing children.

Without the captions and the dotted pattern of the newspaper images, one might take the images for the work of a Conceptual artist with a documentary approach who is engaging in an exploration of urban gray zones. Given that Piller reproduces images that have already been reproduced, using the term "photography" to describe his work is as imprecise as using it in relation to the diverse range of analogue and digitally produced images that we encounter today and that in many cases look like classical photographs, at best. Even before the emergence of digital images it was logical to view photography as a form of reproductive print, as did William M. Ivins, Jr., in his book *Prints and Visual Communications* first published in 1953.[1]

Juxtaposing reproductions is what brings repeating basic motifs and similarities to light,[2] as does Peter Piller in filtering the images found in regional newspapers. This also applies to details that first become evident when Piller digitally scans the images and enlarges them substantially for exhibition purposes.

He never alters the given motif, because he values the "virtues of the unintentional."[3] Beyond the intentions of those who created the photograph, he manages to distill an astoundingly precise and coherent iconography, which has become widely prevalent – for the most part unconsciously.

The presentation and publication of Piller's images takes place on three different levels. There is the *Peter Piller Archive* of some 7000 collected images, publications of the archive in book form, and the presentation of larger versions of the images in exhibitions. There is thus no categorical difference between Piller's "work" and the "exhibition." Every viewable presentation is an independent work conceived by the artist in every detail. Consequently, Piller does not produce conventional exhibition catalogues.

Image captions are included in the books published with images from the archive, as in the sizeable volume *Zeitung* (Newspaper), which was published in 2008 and brings together a wide range of image categories. However, captions are not incorporated into exhibitions, and the artist never assigns his own text to an image.

Without the accompanying captions – explaining, for example, that at Denkmalstraße 14 in Günterod an 80-year-old woman was murdered by her own son, whom the police deemed mentally ill, or that Hartmut H. was murdered in the depicted twin house – the *Tatorthäuser* (Houses with Crime Scenes) look like an exemplary collection of nondescript residences.

Piller's investigations also repeatedly lead to *Ungeklärte Fälle* (Unsolved Cases). Under this rubric he collects newspaper photos that do not fit into any other category, or, in other words, for which no other images have been found to group into a category. Lone photographs that do not fit into any one classification are not restricted from the archive but incorporated. Ultimately, all of the categories by which Piller sorts photographs simultaneously serve to demonstrate the limits of categorization.

On the one hand, Piller is interested in the "social uses" of photography, which were studied comprehensively for the first time by Pierre Bourdieu and his researchers in the 1960s in a study commissioned by Kodak.[4] On the other hand, Piller repeatedly emphasizes aspects of his selected images, which an analysis of the social applications of photography would hardly consider, although such elements also potentially have sociological relevance. This is true of the aerial photographs taken by a company in the 1980s as a means of capitalizing on the pride of German homeowners.

Houses from Above

Originally, the photographs of single-family homes and the surrounding properties were nicely framed and offered to the individual owners for sale. In 2002, Piller managed to gain possession of the some 20 000 negatives in the company estate. A portion of the archive of aerial photographs was published in 2004 in a book entitled *Von Erde schöner* (More Beautiful from Earth).[5] As with the photographs from local newspapers, the motifs remain unchanged. Also, the format in which Piller presents the individual, carefully selected photographs in an exhibition context corresponds approximately to the size of the photographs offered for sale by the company. However, Peter Piller adheres even more closely to the "original" than the company did, which often cropped the images to omit unsightly elements in the surroundings or to enhance the appearance of the house; the artist, in turn, always uses the entire image on the negative. Precisely his willingness to forego any interference in the image allows interesting details to surface that the photographer and possibly also the company did not notice. For example, there is a series of photos in which an excavation pit or the foundation of another building under construction can be seen next to the house.

The series *Schlafende Häuser* (Sleeping Houses) is characterized by closed blinds, a lack of people, and other signs indicating the temporary or long-term absence of the inhabitants. A surprising number of photos show houses that seem to be sticking out their tongues in *Zungen* (Tongues), whereby red sheets and quilts have been hung out the window for airing out. Other categories into which Piller has grouped photographs in series or thematic collections include *Pfade* (Paths), *Pool, Mensch vor Haus* (Person in Front of Building), *Gemähter Rasen* (Mowed Grass). Other photographs show soccer fields, camping sites, birds flying across the picture, and sooty clouds – all things that must not have played a significant role in the reasoning behind the production of the photograph. Only through Piller's compilation do the cement slab paths leading across the grass become an interesting study on the geometric patterns of straight or curved, branching or crossing lines, which seem to reflect the psychological disposition of the individual inhabitants.

Lending a structured order to the overabundance of material was anything but easy. As with the images from local newspapers, Piller's classifications almost seem surrealistic. One might even feel tempted to recall the Chinese encyclopedia and its list of "arbitraries" described by the Argentine author Jorge Luis Borges when arguing: "It is clear that there is no classification of the Universe not being arbitrary and full of conjectures."[6]

Who Is the Conceptual Artist?

Underlying the almost matter-of-fact classifications and categorizations that Piller applies to his collection of images is a fundamental skepticism as to whether the organization of the material leads to any kind of essential statement about the nature of the world. "I am not concerned with the truth. My archive is not objective," stated Piller in an interview in 2004,[7] for which the editorial commentary introduces Piller as a "Conceptual artist." This is accurate only to a limited extent. The formulation of the *taz* newspaper that "the concept is the art" does not apply, and herein lies the key difference between Piller's approach and that of "classic" Conceptual artists. Even the art journal *Texte zur Kunst*, which is generally concerned with delivering a good degree of theoretical precision, features a review from 2011 claiming that the "Conceptual artist from Hamburg" had become known for salvaging and arranging a pool of found images,[8] but not questioning the term "Conceptual artist" to any extent.

An interesting comparison is offered by the "archive" of 34 aerial photographs that Ed Ruscha commissioned in 1967 of parking lots in the larger metropolitan area of Los Angeles. For this *Thirtyfour Parking Lots* series, Ruscha engaged a photographer to take black-and-white photographs from a helicopter. The "Conceptual" idea of photographing 34 parking lots from above could have been carried out in different ways, and Ruscha himself said that he did not know whether in this project he was more interested in the regular linear patterns of the parking places or the pattern of the oil stains.[9]

Like Peter Piller, Ed Ruscha acts as an observer of the given material, which, as in the photographs of the single-family homes, reveals surprising details and aesthetic qualities. However, he gave himself a set of rules, which allowed for variations in terms of execution and resulted in a number of surprises for the artist. If the idea had never been carried out, one could have viewed the "instructions" as a conceptual concept, as the actual work of art. This notion is indispensable to other conceptual approaches, such as that of Douglas Huebler's work *Variable Piece No. 70*, also known as *Everyone Alive*, which was initiated in 1971. Huebler's intention, which he put into writing, was to "photographically document, to the extent of his capacity ... the existence of everyone alive in order to produce the most authentic and inclusive representation of the human species that may be assembled in this manner."[10] The project was, of course, nowhere near completion at the time of the artist's death in 1997.

Is Piller's approach at all comparable to that of the classic Conceptual artist? Is his working process not more like the "concept" of the company that had the aerial photographs systematically and, to an extent, mechanically produced[11] – but taking this to a point of absurdity? When Piller received the aerial photographs he first had no idea what to do with them but combed through the almost unmanageable amount of images again and again, for months on end, until systematic categories subsequently crystalized.

The situation of the photographs excerpted from local newspapers is similar. The *Bauerwartungsflächen* "indexically"[12] refer to planned residential complexes or supermarkets, but as a result not of Piller's concept but of the "Conceptual" approach shared by municipalities and investors.

While Driving Past

The term Conceptual Art would apply most readily to later photo series, in which Piller himself took up the camera or had someone else take photographs. From 2007 to 2011, Piller stringently executed a concept on his regular drives from his home in Hamburg to his teaching position in Leipzig. Each time that he passed Bad Fallingbostel on the A7 autobahn running through the Lüneburger Heath, he took a color photograph from the car of the logo of the Kraft food company, which could be seen from a distance. The variety of these individual photographs is based on the time of day, the given weather conditions, and the speed at which he passed the logo. The blurry photographs have a painterly quality, and the letters on the logo are often only faintly decipherable, contrasting with the semantics of *Kraft* as "strength" in German. These photographs hardly correspond with the common standards of "Conceptual" photography, as defined by an almost documentary, sober clarity. Instead, the *Kraft* series tends to recall Impressionist painting series by Claude Monet, such as the façade of the Rouen Cathedral, haystacks, and the water lilies in his garden in Giverny, all captured at different times of day and in different lighting situations.[13]

Kraft was published in book form and is presented as a slide show in exhibitions. Unforeseen by the artist, the series also documented a piece of history. The striking logo in Bad Fallingbostel was removed in 2012, when the multinational was divided into two independent companies, now bearing the less evocative name of Mondelēz International outside of North America.

Ultimately, chance factors more significantly than concept. In 2011, Piller's eight-year-old son had this idea of photographing his father while asleep. This resulted in 38 photographs undermining any and every standard of professional photography and conveying an almost touching sense of intimacy. Are they not also an ironic swan song to the classical notion of artistic genius, who seeks inspiration, so to speak, while sleeping? At any rate, these are fitting "self-portraits" of an artist whose own activities always take place in the background, behind the images that he puts forward. Piller is less an image-maker than a subjective image-collector or image-selector. The individuality of his approach lies not in a certain style or gesture but in the specific manner in which he forms new relationships between images. Peter Piller does not follow any predetermined concept or formula but instead makes a very conscious selection, in contrast to Huebler, for example. He proceeds in the manner of a search engine, not only operating within the fathomless dimensions of the Internet but also, and for the most part, in the gray, in-between zones of analogue reality. Are perhaps the *Suchende Polizisten* (Police Searching) from the local papers, who are shown combing through fields or inspecting dirt roads, something of an alter ego for an artist who scours his pool of images?

The Genre of the Photography Collection

The British art historian David Sylvester once remarked: "One of the strengths of artists in all media in the second half of the twentieth century has been that less *intervention* is more."[14] This is also true of Peter Piller, whose work is thoroughly indebted to an honored tradition of non-intervention, that is, of using found material. Piller is not the first photograph collector in recent art history. His work can be viewed as aligned with the tradition of an artistic style or genre that has become increasingly established since the 1960s. It essentially consists of developing formats for the presentation of collected materials and could be roughly labeled as the "photography collection." Found photographs, images cut from newspapers, magazines, or books, photos taken by the artist or, since the existence of the Internet, excerpted from the digital universe, and reproduced photographs are presented in stringent series or also in highly unusual constellations and sequences.

Such works range from Bernd and Hilla Becher's systematic photographic archiving of obsolete industrial architecture, to the *Section Publicité* on the motif of the eagle in Marcel Broodthaers's fictitious Musée d'Art Moderne, Gerhard

Richter's comprehensive collection of photographs entitled *Atlas,* Christian Boltanski's fictive reconstruction of his own childhood in photographs, and Hans-Peter Feldmann's celebration of the everyday photographic production of ordinary people.

In 1997, Benjamin H.D. Buchloh was the first to examine the "genre" of the photography collection in contemporary art as a cohesive subject of study. In many cases he observed an "almost mechanical arrangement, like that found in the system of the archive."[15] The extensive use of found photographs and printed reproductions was already present in the collages and montages of the 1920s and 1930s. However, a difference between these and later practices was that the images present in the "photography collections" were usually used completely, and not just cut-out parts or motifs thereof. In addition, in contrast to the confrontational and shocking aesthetic of montage, the images tend to be presented in some kind of serial organization and fluid or network-like branching structure. Also, according to Buchloh, aspects of content that come to bear in the "photography collections," such as the "recording of complex historical processes, the amassing of facts, the arrangement of events in chronological order and temporal continuity," fundamentally contradict the "the avant-garde objectives for immediacy, shock, and fragmentation."[16] Also, Piller's compilations subscribe less to an aesthetic of shock than of continuity. In his investigation, Buchloh concentrated on European artists and thus did not discuss the Appropriation Art practices found in the United States, which around 1980 further developed the borrowing of found images into a programmatic "postmodern" subversion of traditional models of originality and authorship.

Like Louise Lawler and Sherrie Levine, Richard Prince inverted the classic relationship between original, copy, and fake. As in the case of Piller, a job dealing with images provided the initial spark for his artistic approach to photography. Prince had worked in the "tear sheets" department of Time Life since 1976.[17]

Prince reworked advertising images, such as the Marlboro cowboy or sexist depictions in motorcycle magazines through a series of processes that avoided any indication of a traditional artistic hand: "The photographs were excerpted from the originals, with a pair of scissors or through the use of a camera, which Prince called 'electronic scissors.' He views the copying process as 8-track photography, in the sense of a synchronized music recording . . . . Working from an original, which is itself a copy, Prince explores the acceptance for the copying process as an artistic practice, which is limited to the manipulation of the cut-out, the color, and sharpness of the image."[18]

The changes made to the original by Prince go much farther than in the case of Piller. Like Pop Art artists, Prince shows a preference for motifs that have become anchored in social memory through their presence in advertising and mass media, which he deconstructs through his manipulation of the image.

The resulting images always convey a tension between the original and the altered image – a tension absent in the work of Piller, to the extent that he prefers to work with images that originate from a context of social use but only enter into a more widespread consciousness through his artistic selection and emphasis.

Both in the work of Prince and in that of Piller is manifested something that one could describe as social or cultural visual memory. Prince "portraits" social groups, which tend to exist in the given form only in rural areas of the United States, whereas Piller's motifs are closely linked to the milieus of small towns or suburbia in German-speaking regions. What are the artists' attitudes toward these various milieus? More articulated in the work of Piller than of Prince is a sense of distance infused with subtle irony, through which the material also takes on humorous aspects without indicating a clear stance toward the various social contexts portrayed.

Invisible Damage

"Is Peter Piller a mean-spirited cynic, who makes the petty bourgeoisie look ridiculous, or is he acting out of sympathy?" asks Till Briegleb in his review of Piller's exhibition at Kunstverein Braunschweig in 2011. This show included photographs of damages that had been submitted to Basler Versicherungen (an insurance company) as part of a claim. In 2007 Piller was given access to the digital archive of the insurer, from which he selected 48 photographs, which he shows in alternating selections in exhibitions. According to Briegleb, the "amateur photo documentation" from the archive of the insurance company gives rise to the "sense that one is being confronted with a good, sardonic dose of denunciation." The images, "for all their humor, . . . are also spiteful. A giant red, patent-leather shoe protrudes into the picture, although the image is documenting a small water stain with tiles . . . and on many photographs it is simply impossible to identify what is actually broken."[19]

Briegleb is at least suggesting the possibility of interpreting Piller's approach as stemming from an arrogance, rooted in social superiority, toward the unguided forms of expression of the lower classes. But is Piller's work not more indebted to the larcenous pleasure of the forger and manipulator, who acts as if he had done nothing wrong but has in truth secretly changed everything? And haven't his images to a certain extent become liberated from their creators and context of application, when Piller uses them to almost fundamentally demonstrate how photography can show much but often not what is crucial or intended?

The definition of what makes photography art, also in the context of the comprehensive activities of artists like Peter Piller, has shifted decidedly. No longer is it essential that a photograph "look like art" or not. Its artistic relevance is measured more or less by the extent to which it fails to show or else misrepresents something in an interesting way – something that one would expect from the "social use" of photographs or what one commonly calls by that name. Piller thus draws us into the dialectic and even paradoxical relationship between the visible and the invisible.

1 William M. Ivins, Jr., *Prints and Visual Communications*, MIT Press, Cambridge, MA, 1953.
2 On the current and historical significance of Aby Warburg's *Mnemosyne Atlas* in this context, see my essay "Space for thinking between the images: On the genesis of the 'photographic collection' as an artistic genre," in: Eva Schmidt and Ines Rüttinger (eds.), *Dear Aby Warburg: What can be done with images? Dealing with photographic material*, exhib. cat. Museum für Gegenwartskunst Siegen, Kehrer, Heidelberg, 2012, pp. 26–35.
3 The German original reads *Vorzüge der Absichtslosigkeit*, which was the title of an exhibition by Peter Piller at the Museum für Gegenwartskunst in Siegen (2004) and is also the title for all his public lectures.
4 See Pierre Bourdieu, *Photography: A Middle-brow Art*, Stanford University Press, Stanford, 1990, p. 74. Originally published in French in 1965.
5 *Von Erde schöner* was published by Revolver Verlag, Frankfurt am Main, 2004. Since 2002 the publishing house has been releasing series of regional newspaper photographs from Peter Piller's archive and plans to produce approximately twenty volumes.
6 The English translation stems from: Jorge Luis Borges, "The Analytical Language of John Wilkins," trans. Lilia Graciela Vázquez, available online at: www.alamut.com/subj/artiface/language/johnWilkins.html, accessed 09/04/2014. This essay was also published in: Jorge Luis Borges, *Other Inquisitions 1937–1952*, trans. Ruth L. C. Simms, University of Texas Press, Austin, 1964.
7 "Es geht nicht um die Wahrheit." Martin Droschke interviews Peter Piller, in: *die tageszeitung*, July 6, 2004, p. 15.
8 Eric Aichinger, *Ruhe und Kraft: Über Peter Piller in der Galerie Barbara Wien/Wilma Lukatsch, Berlin*, www.textezurkunst.de/daily/2011/mar/29/eric-aichinger-peter-piller-barbara-wien-de/, accessed 09/06/2014. The article is imprecise in other regards. The photographs from local newspapers are described as "stock photography," which would indicate that the newspapers garnered their photographs from an archive containing optimally neutral images that can be used for a range of purposes instead of sending photographers to the actual sites of regional events.
9 Quoted in: *Monets Vermächtnis*, exhib. cat. Hamburger Kunsthalle, Hatje Cantz, Ostfildern, 2001, p. 150.
10 Peter Osborne (ed.), *Conceptual Art*, Phaidon, London and New York, 2002, p. 83.

11 "The idea becomes a machine that makes art," wrote Sol Lewitt in 1967 in a seminal text on the early use of the term, "Paragraphs on Conceptual Art" published in 1967 in *Artforum*. Quoted in: Tony Godfrey, *Conceptual Art*, Phaidon, London, 1998, p. 13.

12 Can the predominance of the indexical in more recent art be ascribed to photography replacing painting as the model notion of the image? As curator of the 1994 exhibition *Kontext Kunst*, Peter Weibel wrote in the accompanying catalogue that, since Rosalind Krauss's article "Notes on the Index: Seventies Art in America" (1977), "the indexical nature of photography has become a model for postmodern works of art." *Kontext Kunst*, DuMont, Cologne, 1994, p. 40.

13 In her essay "The Originality of the Avant-Garde," Rosalind Krauss describes Claude Monet's seemingly spontaneous brushstroke, and his work on multiple canvases in parallel, as the systematic execution of a concept that merely suggests spontaneity. See Rosalind E. Krauss, *The Originality of the Avant-Garde and Other Modernist Myths*, MIT Press, Cambridge, MA, 1986, p. 167.

14 David Sylvester, *About Modern Art*, Chatto & Windus, London, 1996, p. 389; the author's emphasis.

15 Benjamin H. D. Buchloh, "Warburg's Paragon? The End of Collage and Photomontage in Postwar Europe," in: Ingrid Schaffner and Matthias Winzen (eds.), *Deep Storage: Collection, Storing and Archiving in Art*, exhib. cat. Haus der Kunst, Munich, et al., Prestel, Munich and New York, 1997, pp. 50–60, esp. p. 59.

16 Ibid., p. 50.

17 Richard Prince interviewed by Larry Clark in: Lisa Phillips (ed.), *Richard Prince*, exhib. cat. Whitney Museum of American Art, New York, Harry N. Abrams, New York, 1992, p. 129.

18 Stefan Römer, *Künstlerische Strategien des Fake: Kritik von Fälschung und Original*, DuMont, Cologne, 2001, p. 123.

19 Till Briegleb, "Auf Suche jenseits der Gartenzäune: Macht er das Kleinbürgertum lächerlich oder feiert er es? Die Arbeiten des Künstlers Peter Piller in Braunschweig," in: *Süddeutsche Zeitung*, August 6, 2011.

The Gaze without Intention
On Peter Piller's *Periphery Walks*

Max Küng

"Dakderrigigigi dik-dik," says the blackbird.
"Tew-ip tew-ip tew-ip – tidic-tew tidic-tew tidic-tew – tidic tidic tidic," sings the song thrush.
"Brrrrrrrt," warns the starling.

There is a certain irony in the fact that our biology teacher's name was Herr Vögeli, or Mr. Bird – and that he had a beaky nose on which his thick-rimmed spectacles perched beneath eyebrows like the feathered tufts of a Stygian owl. He looked for all the world as if he were wearing one of those joke false-nose-and-glasses combinations you might find in a party cracker and put on after downing a few drinks. But our teacher Mr. Bird was a rather sober type and, as his name suggests, his favorite creature of all creatures was the bird in every shape, size, form, and species – all ten thousand of them.

Our teacher was a keen, indeed almost evangelical, ornithologist. And so we would trudge along on excursions into the forest at silly-o'clock in the morning, having already been subjected to hours of theoretical birdcall training on tape.

But the forest was dark. And the hour was early. And our young minds were filled with many thoughts that had nothing whatsoever to do with our little feathered friends. How I would love to know now what I saw back then. I saw everything except birds. I heard everything except birds. The very sole of my own shoe was probably of more interest to me than whatever bird our Mr. Bird was pointing out to us – lifting his index finger to his lips to admonish us into silence, then stretching that same finger toward the dense foliage of the forest, into which we all stared, only to see nothing but trees.

"Kseep-kseep-kseep tchirrrr tew-tew-tew duit tchipp-tchipp-tchipp-tchipp tewrtewrtewr tewrrrrrr," trills the chaffinch.
"Bit-bit," says the bullfinch.
"Di-wit-wit di-wit-wit," implore the young goldfinches.

Our teacher Mr. Bird sprang to mind the moment I saw Peter Piller's photographs taken on his walks around the outskirts of the city of Winterthur. Because what all of those photographs have in common is that you can see a bird in them. Sitting on a fence, or on a rooftop. Flying in the air. Up close, far away; sometimes in the middle of the image like its main protagonist, sometimes at the edge, sometimes hidden.

"Tchirr teeteetee," calls the black redstart, and then adds
"krchrch-tewteeteetee."
"Tewli – tri-tri-ti – tri-lui-dididi-tridi," sings the common redstart,
and sometimes "hewit-tick-tick" or "fewit-tek-tek."
"Tsitsitsitsiatsiatsoritiu-tsip," warbles the chaffinch.

Wandering on the periphery has always been an element of Peter Piller's work. Even as a student, back in 1994, he pulled on sturdy shoes and walked the periphery of Hamburg in 26 one-day stages. He encircled the city with the tools of his trade, recording his commentary about what he saw onto a dictaphone – like agent Dale Cooper in *Twin Peaks* constantly communicating with his secretary and reporting everything from the sublime to the ridiculous: "Diane, 2:15 in the afternoon, February 24th. Entering town of Twin Peaks. Never seen so many trees in my life. Lunch was $6.31 and I left her a dollar tip. That was a tuna-fish sandwich on whole wheat and a slice of cherry pie and coffee. Damn good food. And if you ever get up this way, Diane, that cherry pie is worth a stop." Which, in turn, reminds me of Robert Walser, who did not speak into a dictaphone, but who dictated through his pen every detail he absorbed on the walks he enjoyed so much: "and on past shops: stationers, butchers, watchmakers, cobblers, hatters, ironmongers, drapers, grocers, spice merchants, fancy goods, haberdashers, bakers and confectioners. And everywhere, on all these things, the lovely evening sun. As well as lots of noise and bustle, pupils and teachers, the latter with a mien of gravitas and dignity; landscape, fresh air, and much painting." Some time later, he undertook another *Peripheriewanderung* (Periphery Walk) around the Ruhr industrial area. And then around other urban conglomerations. But Peter Piller also documented his walk photographically (walking as a serious undertaking, in contrast to a brief and leisurely stroll – as though the two were unequal siblings: the honest worker versus the charming layabout), and later, in his studio, in the form of drawings created from memory.

"Tchit-tchittchit," beckons the serin.
"Tseeht," calls the dunnock.
"Tsi-da . . . tsi-da . . . tsi-da," says the great tit.

Journeying on foot around a densely populated urban area through a zone that is neither one thing nor another is what interests Peter Piller: the margins, the fringes, neither urban nor rural, but where both dissolve and at the same time converge. The beginning of civilization, the end of nature, and vice versa. And because it is neither one nor the other, it is: nothingness. Or near-nothingness. Or as little as possible. Peter Piller's peripheral walks have a spiritual kinship with the *Siedlungen. Agglomeration* (Settlements. Agglomeration) series by Peter Fischli and David Weiss, in which they soberly, even solemnly, celebrate both the dullness and the sheen of the suburban.

Anyone on foot knows that walking is a good speed at which to see and perceive things, just as Annemarie and Lucius Burckhardt outlined in their "promenadology" or "strollology" of the early 1980s. The aim of their strollology was to achieve a more focused and more aware perception of the wider world, and to extend mere seeing to the point of recognition through walking – as a kind of self-awareness about technocratically determined pen pushers in the world of planners and architects.

"TchiTchiTCHI TchiTchiTCHI," sings the nuthatch.
"Wi-di wii-di wii-di wii widi wii," trills the chiffchaff, and
"tsilp-tsalp-tselp-tsilp-tsalp."
The first verse of the wood warbler's song is like a sewing
machine starting up, and the second goes "tew-tew-tew."

Just as the ethnologies studies in the field, so too does Peter Piller walk the terrain and the grounds he is studying, but he does so erratically, guided more by instinct than by a compass. For his *Peripheriewanderung* around Winterthur, undertaken in two stages in 2013 and 2014, Piller developed a technique that lets us see things we would not otherwise see. Yes, we see birds. In every picture. That lends the series strong cohesion. But we also see everything else that we would not see if we did not see the birds. As so often in a series, the viewer is drawn into a game. Or rather, those viewers still in touch with their inner child. The game is: Can you find the bird in the picture? Where is it? Where is it hiding? But then, just as soon as you find the bird, which disappears by dint of the fact that it is seen, the second image emerges, which is the image of everything-except-the-bird. The bird was the trigger for the trigger, but the bird is also a useful idiot, because it is not about the bird in these pictures, but about everything else. Peter Piller's works conjure a gaze without intention, free of compositional will, unadulterated by good taste. It is a gaze that is neither compassionate nor critical; it is emancipated, with a freedom we have long since lost, perhaps even in childhood. According to Lucius Burckhardt: "Landscape is invisible the way language is inaudible; only colors and sounds are visible and audible, but the effects they generate in the senses of those who perceive them are yet to be fathomed. Is it a coincidence that the earliest landscape descriptions were by a blind man – Homer?"

What did I see back then? As a child in the forest with an unspoiled eye, and virtually blind. I saw what I wanted to. Because I could. Back then, still.

The length of the pause between the "chiz-iz-iz-iz-iz-iz" and the
"zeeeeh" tells us the age of the yellowhammer.
"Tchek-tchek-tchek . . . ," clucks the garden warbler.
"Tew-delew-ew-lio," flutes the golden oriole.

Piller Porn

Notes on Digital *Schaulust*

Dieter Roelstraete

While Peter Piller as a photo artist is not primarily known for self-made photographs, he does occasionally shoot his own pictures, some of which will be shown in the exhibition at Fotomuseum Winterthur. More frequently he works with other people's photographs – more pointedly: with *nobody's* photographs, that is to say, with the anonymous "found footage" of the unidentifiable everyman (the gendered specificity of that word is not without significance here). Peter Piller is perhaps perfectly placed to comment on the vertiginous visuality of our contemporary digital lifeworld. This world is a fully mediated multiverse that is almost entirely made up of incessantly recycled, secondhand images, and home to a regime that has an especially charged relationship with the taboo-tended topic of human sexual behavior in particular.

A mind-boggling statistic, culled from a BBC web page dated (that is to say, *outdated*) June 30, 2013, reads: "according to estimates from [the] Scandinavian research center Sintef, 90% of all the data the human race has ever produced has been generated in the past two years" – an explosion that is primarily "due to the rise of the web, smartphones, social media and the 'big data' projects in which businesses, governments and scientists are involved."[1] Inevitably, anyone interested in the black hole that is the Internet – or maybe it's just me: "sex" was definitely the first word I ever typed into a search engine the first time I surfed the World Wide Web sometime in those innocuous early 1990s – will want to know how much of those data are "not safe for work," that is to say, of a pornographic nature. On a related note: "according to the Planck mission team, and based on the standard model of cosmology, the total mass-energy of the known universe contains 4.9% ordinary matter, 26.8% dark matter and 68.3% dark energy. Thus, dark matter is estimated to constitute 84.5% of the total matter in the universe, while dark energy plus dark matter constitute 95.1% of the total content of the universe."[2] Compare this to the numbers game undergirding the so-called Deepnet, Hidden Web, or Invisible Web – that part of the World Wide Web that is not part of the Surface Web we know so well through our standard search engines: "according to Bright Planet, a search organization specializing in Invisible Web content extraction, the Invisible Web contains nearly 550 billion individual documents compared to the one billion of the surface Web."[3] Cue and enter Peter Piller's photo series *Internetzugang* (Internet Access) . . .

Indeed, it may sometimes appear as if the Internet, as a quintessentially *visual* technology – its skeleton made up, appropriately, of *optical* fiber cables – were pretty much invented for the sole purpose of allowing the boundless proliferation, and global dissemination, of pictures of naked people, men and women alike, in varying states of erotic arousal, for the joys of showing and seeing. These are matters of great interest to artists such as Peter Piller, scavengers of the visible world. One can only guess what Sigmund Freud would have made of it, he who was the first to theorize both the impulse to look, see, watch and the libidinous pleasure derived from it, calling this *Schaulust* (or, more technically and less poetically, scopophilia), one of the cornerstones of human sexual experience.

On the subject of *Schaulust*, Freud noted the following in his groundbreaking "Three Essays on the Theory of Sexuality" from 1905:

> Visual impressions remain the most frequent pathway along which libidinal excitation is aroused; indeed, natural selection counts upon the accessibility of this pathway – if such a teleological form of statement is permissible – when it encourages the development of beauty in the sexual object. The progressive concealment of the body which goes along with civilization keeps sexual curiosity awake. This curiosity seeks to complete the sexual object by revealing its hidden parts. It can, however, be diverted ("sublimated") in the direction of art, if its interest can be shifted away from the genitals on to the shape of the body as a whole.[4]

In fact, it is here, in the very first mention of the mechanics of sublimation in the entire Freud corpus, that the groundwork is laid for the development, only much later, of a properly psychoanalytic theory of art – art as a tactic of *diversion* for the roving, perennially sex-starved eye; art as a variant of the aforementioned game of seeing and being seen, showing and being shown. Decades later, Jacques Lacan refined Freud's theory of *Schaulust* in his *Four Fundamental Concepts of Psycho-Analysis*, noting tersely that "the root of the scopic drive is to be found entirely in the subject, in the fact that *the subject sees himself.*"[5] Visual pleasure, in other words, is not merely a matter of me seeing you (him seeing her, in most cases). It is perhaps above all a matter of me seeing myself – or rather, me seeing myself looking at her, me enjoying the spectacle of my looking at her. My pleasure, experienced vicariously – namely, in a visual *record* of that pleasure. (This, to me, seems to be the causal ghost in the machine of the hugely prolific "amateur" porn industry: not so much the shared joy of sex, but rather the shared joy of looking at ourselves supposedly enjoying sex. But I digress.) It is this cascading tangle of ocular *mise en abyme* that the Internet has exploded with such singular force, its featureless margins trawled by Piller's eye.

Speaking of featureless margins, of Cyberia's defeatured outback: *Hintergrundfarben* (Background Colors) is a series of photographs – screenshots, to be more precise – depicting empty chat rooms. With the rooms' (typically) sparsely clad female occupants gone (for a cigarette break, for lunch, for a quick trip to the toilet, for the day – who keeps time, online?), our probing gaze is left to scan the dour monochromatic expanses of the poky rooms in question, with their fraying curtains, lightly crumpled bedsheets, the pastel edge of a sofa stationed in a nameless building somewhere in . . . Sofia? Reno? Mannheim? The *banlieues* of Paris? (Not so much the middle of, but plainly, nowhere.) A dispassionate exploration of the various non-places and non-sites that constitute the everyday, modern love life of the World Wide Web, *Hintergrundfarben* simultaneously occupies a place in the more art-historically minded end of the Piller scale. While the title may allude to the ubiquitous scourge of Photoshop technology, the series' deadpan visual content unwittingly invokes shades of pictorial quasi-abstraction in manners both grand (Barnett Newman, Mark Rothko) and mundane (Gerhard Richter, Luc Tuymans). All in all, this is a small comfort, evidently, for the glaring absence of the photo series' real subjects: missing women, elliptical girls. So much for *Schaulust*!

In *Frau Baum* (Mrs. Baum), Piller's Cyberian women edge closer to the edge of visibility – yet ultimately remain ghoulish digital ciphers. The pictures in this series were taken from run-of-the-mill dating sites. All of the (young) women in them are shown leaning on or against trees. Nothing necessarily phallic – nothing as phallic as the object attachments portrayed in *Schießende Mädchen* (*Shooting Girls*) and *Eis essende Mädchen* (Girls Eating Ice Cream), say. Though the glassy filter of a bathroom window through which we appear to be seeing these women may perhaps be read as a knowing nod to the soft-focus photo aesthetic of earlier, slightly more innocent *artes eroticae* – think David Hamilton or Bob Guccione and 1970s Penthouse. Such innuendo, echoing the culture of the namelessness, doubling, and anonymity typical of Internet culture, is defiantly cast aside in the self-explanatory series of newspaper photographs *Eis essende Mädchen*, depicting young women enthusiastically licking ice-cream cones (one looking absurdly, outlandishly big). Of the gun-toting, shooting women captured in *Schießende Mädchen*, the artist has observed, in an e-mail exchange with the author, that "girls are more frightening, aren't they?" (In said conversation, Piller also noted how "only every 50th or 100th image of somebody with a weapon in German newspapers shows a girl." And how "there is no group of shooting men in my archive.") Women posing, and women caught in the act; women self-consciously facing the camera, and women as the unwitting objects of the mass media's machinic gaze; absent women, whose empty quarters return our frustrated stares: all variations on the demonic dance of seeing and being seen, which the advent of the World Wide Web has cast in such dramatic new light – though one that keeps its focus firmly fixed on the female form first and foremost, the tried and tested site of *Schaulust* old and new.

By way of conclusion: one "portrait of a lady" by Peter Piller, haunted by the specter of Edward Snowden – shorthand, since mid-2013, for the massive surveillance apparatus we always knew was deeply embedded in our techno-world – adds a dimly political edge to this whole (mostly frivolous, only occasionally lugubrious) *Schaulust* business. It is an image taken from the artist's series *Von Erde schöner* (More Beautiful from Earth), a collection of literally hundreds of aerial photographs of suburban dream houses originally produced for commercial purposes (prophetic shades, here, of the global economic crises of recent years, brought on by one real-estate bubble too many). In fact, it is the image that graces the very cover of the lavish book in which all of these photographs have been neatly compiled: a nondescript house, set in not terribly charming semi-rural environs, with a pale-looking woman (girl?) lounging on a terrace in the sun. She is wearing what looks like a red top and pinkish panties, but that's basically as much as I am able to make out from the digital file the artist sent me "for research purposes." As I open the file, I inevitably find myself zooming in on the figure of the scantily clothed damsel, so blissfully unaware of the spying eye above her, but the image quickly dissolves in a jarring mosaic of pixels, the zeroes and ones of Cyberian lore. There is nothing to see here.

1 Mark Ward, "Web porn: Just how much is there?," *BBC News*, available online at: www.bbc.com/news/technology-23030090, accessed 09/02/2014.

2 "Dark Matter," BBC website, www.bbc.co.uk/science/space/universe/questions.../dark_matter, accessed 09/02/2014.

3 Wendy Boswell, "How big is the Invisible Web?," About.com, websearch.about.com/od/invisibleweb/f/What-Is-The-Size-Of-The-Hidden-Web.htm, accessed 09/02/2014.

4 Sigmund Freud, "Three Essays on the Theory of Sexuality," in: *On Sexuality*, Penguin Books, Harmondsworth and New York, 1977 (1905), p. 69.

5 Jacques Lacan, *The Four Fundamental Concepts of Psycho-Analysis*, W. W. Norton, New York, 1978, p. 194; the italics are mine, DR.

What Remains of the Image

A Juxtaposition of Disparate Elements

Maren Lübbke-Tidow

> *Yes, I have always said that, with any sculpture, you have to be able to say, although this is not a readymade, it could be one. That's what a sculpture is supposed to look like. It must have a certain relation to reality. I mean, not airy-fairy, let alone fabricated, so aloof and polite . . . . And I don't see this aspect in many artists' works. Often, my feeling is that they think something up that is supposed to be art. That's not what I want at all. Rather, a sculpture is really a photo – although it can be shifted, it must still always have an aspect that reality has too.*
>
> Isa Genzken

It is worthwhile to examine the work of Peter Piller in the context of the debates surrounding the dispositifs of archiving and reworking photographs as currently manifested in contemporary artistic practices. Since the mid-1990s, he has been exploring the field of different cultural and social practices and areas of activity in which photography serves a mediating function. Piller forms his own visual constellations by examining existing, found, and sought-out images. Yet at the same time, through the manner in which he reconfigures these materials, he suggests new ways of reading them. His artistic work – encompassing his artist books as well as his presentation concepts for exhibitions – is indebted to an analytical approach. His works are a very particular form of media reflection. In this sense, Piller draws on a central paradigm of the art of the twentieth century – Conceptual Art – and develops his visual strategies from it. This also suggests some promising insights into how the paradigms guiding conceptually informed processes have shifted and into what role the works of Peter Piller have come to play in this context. Core debates about art have long since ceased to center on a departure from the image, liberation from the object, and evading the commercialization of art; at issue instead is the fundamental tension between concept and image, between the visible and representation, and between methodology and meaning. In his extensive *Peter Piller Archive*, the artist investigates the fundamental disposition of photography as a technique for showing and seeing.

What (initially) becomes evident in the series of works that he has developed from the archive is a critical and contradictory relationship to the visual that calls into question the event-like nature or documentality (Hito Steyerl) of the photographic image.

In the *Zeitung* (Newspaper) segment of the *Peter Piller Archive*, he achieves this, for example, by processing a phenomenology of regional events, rituals, and ceremonies. This is based on a collection of photographs published in local newspapers – whose principles of composition seem to follow an unstated set of formal rules. His practice of collecting and using utilitarian photographs is often compared with that of Hans-Peter Feldmann. However, up to now, I have only found the obsessive nature characterizing Peter Piller's work as a whole, and this project in particular, in a comparable form in the work of artist and healer Marianne Wex, who, in the years between 1972 and 1977, collected over 5 000 photographic reproductions for her project *Weibliche und männliche Körpersprache als Folge patriarchalischer Machtverhältnisse* (Let's Take Back Our Space: "Male" and "Female" Body Language as a Result of Patriarchal Structures). In a book of the same title published in 1979, she compiled them into a typology of poses, through which she attempted to demonstrate the difference between the sexes. Coinciding with the rise of theoretical debates (in Europe) around the constructed nature of the photographic image, this work by Marianne Wex formed a basis or point of reference for many woman artists, who subsequently also explored representations of the (female) body in the media. Today – some three decades later and with reference to another debate – Piller is able to use a different point of departure. Like the work of Wex, his complete *Peter Piller Archive* and the *Zeitung* segment thereof are also organized in categories not only encompassing certain themes, but above all, incorporating various specific compositional logics. *Zeitung* shows the almost ritual repetition of formalized and standardized news photographs in daily newspapers accompanying specific events of largely regional significance. They attest to certain representational conventions, as Marianne Wex already observed, although Piller pursued a completely different, one might say more banal thematic focus and, above all, has taken a decidedly critical approach to the documentary photographic image. His different categories emphatically express that past notions about forms of visual (i.e., photographic) authentication no longer apply. His phenomenology of regional events, rituals, and ceremonies simultaneously becomes a phenomenology of their visual representation, which he relishes in unmasking as fiction. Peter Piller maintains a tension in his series – and this applies to all the images in the *Peter Piller Archive* – between the visual document and the fictional moment inscribed in it. This is the potential with which he works. The lyrical quality of the titles that he assigns to his categories, which are often derived from the actual captions of the images, cultivates this potential of fictionalization and at the same time lends his work an open, fleet-footed character.

In contrast to many of his colleagues working on the interfaces between the documentary and the fictional, Peter Piller refuses – and to me this seems important to the considerations that follow – to present this critical and contradictory relationship to the visual as a kind of *crisis* of the photographic (documentary) image. He instead offensively and ecstatically clings to the visuality of the documentary image, still or specifically trying to wring the unusual from the banal image. Instead of "merely" critically addressing the ways in which visual representation functions, he moreover explicitly explores the *expressive* potential of documentary photography, attempting to discover *what remains of an image*, when, having retraced the steps in its making, we come to understand the mechanisms of the way the image generates meaning and factor in its exploitation logic. What is there then left to see in the images? Peter Piller has the unique ability to wrest something from these images and create "something" productive within them, even if they appear utterly hollowed out. This is the point at which he departs from the beaten path of contemporary Conceptual Art – in which the photographic series continues to function as a key variable in a critical but, above all, logical interpretation – and, so to speak, heads into the thicket of the manifold overwritings of photographic images in order to find something else to bring to the surface and give it another space – a type of poetological approach.

Peter Piller would, however, never add anything to the images as a means of providing something "more" to see than is actually shown. On the contrary, his collections of images have the character of a matter-of-fact and dry presentation of things that were once purposely photographed for a specific purpose. At the same time, in the "space" of his books as well as in his exhibitions, he works toward lending the images a kind of *physicality*. The *Peter Piller Archive* not only offers pictures to see but also to *experience.* In an inversion of the introductory quote from Isa Genzken, the images turn into a kind of readymade, not airy-fairy or fabricated, not aloof and polite, but with a certain relation to reality – that then shifts toward something else.

This is as unique to Piller as it is consistent. The archive does not function (any longer) as a storehouse of photographic source material that serves as some kind of objective knowledge or proof. The sheer amount of photographic material with a consistent sameness of visual rhetoric works against conventional forms of perception. Despite its wealth of images, it empties itself entirely on its own. Instead, from each individual series develops a kind of corpus with the potential to distance itself from a clear identification of the objects depicted – a corpus in which each serial stringing-together consistently yields new formations. They retain their mutability because the individual images themselves, as accessible and ordinary as they initially seem, also consistently bear witness to a blithesome, strange, or ominous coexistence of people and things. Whether planned or unplanned, something in the images that does not belong together a priori comes together. Through his processes of selecting and compiling images into categories and series, Piller directs the viewer's gaze toward these curious-ominous and equally fantastical moments. The *Peter Piller Archive* thus has a performative character. It is a speculative project, an appeal to viewers to engage with these compilations. In this sense, I therefore understand Peter Piller's work on the archive not only as a means of working with photographs or with the documentary as a form of critical reflection or political practice, but largely as an investigation into the specific physicality of photographic images.

To a certain extent, the *Archive* articulates the formation of a photographic corpus of images, comparable with the work of a sculptor, who creates a new relationship between forms in order to communicate a specifically physical, spatially oriented experience to the viewer. The photographs of plots slated for development, in German so-called *Bauerwartungsflächen* (Future Building Sites) which are brought together in the category *Bauerwartungsflächen (Noch ist nichts zu sehen)* (Nothing Yet To Be Seen) would be one example of this, as are *0 bis 100* (0 to 100), *Wilder Müll* (Abandoned Garbage), *Regionales Leuchten* (Local Glow), *Einweihungsbänder* (Ceremonial Ribbons), *Projektionsflächen* (Projection Surfaces), *Bedeutungsflächen* (Surfaces of Meaning), *Schandfleck/Schmuckstück* (Eyesore/Gem), *Vandalismus* (Vandalism), *Gefällt* (Cut Down), *Trist, traurig, trostlos, Tristesse* (Somber, Sad, Bleak, Sadness), and *Ungeklärte Fälle* (Unsolved Cases). At the same time, not only the images from the *Peter Piller Archive: Zeitung* offer themselves up to such an interpretation; many more from the archive as a whole might be added: *Hintergrundfarben* (Background Colors) from the category *Internet* includes such images and in particular also the photographs in the series *Nimmt Schaden* (Suffers Damage) and *Dauerhaftigkeit* (Permanence) as well as certain images from *Von Erde schöner* (More Beautiful from Earth).

With *Peripheriewanderungen* (Periphery Walks) this dimension of a reception directly linked to the physicality of the photographic images is much more palpable. The *Peter Piller Archive*, which works exclusively with found images, is still "photographic" to a certain extent – more photographic than the *Peripheriewanderungen*, which comprise a corpus of images consisting of photographs and drawings by the artist. (Something that is already interesting in and of itself: we would generally ascribe fundamentally higher standards, with respect to the photograph as an image, to photographs by artists than to the image as a utilitarian photograph. But this is merely an aside.) That the images from the *Peter Piller Archive* are more "photographic" is due, on the one hand, to the fact that they offer something clearly identifiable, which is by no means always the case in the *Peripheriewanderungen*. On the other hand, in his *Archive* the fixing of a moment in time is also clearly important – an aspect fundamentally inherent to the photograph and to the archive in particular. In *Peripheriewanderungen*, the fixing of space is shifted above and beyond this fixing of time and – as is underscored by the title of the work and the knowledge of the viewer – it becomes clear that a space was traversed and that the photographs and drawings are thus traces of this experience; temporal axis versus spatial axis, so to speak.

Peter Piller visited the outskirts of various cities and visually documented these areas. His walks around Hamburg, the Ruhr region, Barcelona, Graz, and Bonn have been compiled into series. In doing so, Piller was not concerned with locating the official city limits as indicated on the map, but with discovering and passing through zones where one kind of space transitions into another. If we assume that Peter Piller, with his images from *Peripheriewanderungen*, is not pursuing the idea of systematically gathering information guided by logical parameters in order to, for example, cohesively depict an area, but is instead interested in discovering something that is undefined, that involves something different than his usual perceptions – then, in this case, the outskirts of a city are certainly appropriate areas to explore. Here, one no longer sees anything that might immediately indicate urban life, nor does one see anything that might suggest the notion of rural life. Nevertheless, the images from *Peripheriewanderungen* have characteristic qualities: they reveal a juxtaposition of disparate elements.

As in the *Peter Piller Archive*, the artist also makes productive use of this juxtaposition of disparate elements in *Peripheriewanderungen*. With his camera, he focuses on details, goes between the kinds of phenomena that often appear on the periphery. Things become manifest everywhere and purposefully, and objects are organized in a makeshift manner or painstakingly, seemingly part of a larger plan – a plan to which no one is privy and that therefore can easily be thwarted by other plans. The things do not coalesce; a sense of order and oversight is not asserted. Spaces remain open-ended and largely undefined, or layered over by other spaces that insert themselves in-between. Here, something constantly tries to take form, but ultimately remains unstructured. The view is obscured. It is therefore a superb place for Peter Piller to turn his camera to, as improper as the things there appear. Since here he can impose his own logic onto the images, free of any conventional ascriptions. In his pictures, Piller makes use of this literally improper potential. Thus, in his photographs, unconnected things enter into a liaison, forming a corpus of their own with its own expression. In their compositional logic, the drawings interspersed throughout *Peripheriewanderungen,* and through which the artist recalls what he has seen at times, have a similar function. In this case, however, they follow a similar idea or a similar pattern: recording something that is real because it was seen once, recording something that has a real basis, but is free of the usual attributions. This is what remains of the image. It is this type of figurative nature of documentary images that Piller offers the viewer. "Although this is not a readymade, it could be one. That's what a sculpture has to look like" – this thought comes to me when I look at the photographs from Piller's *Peripheriewanderungen*. This thought is indebted to the physicality of his images, which comes into being when he brings together the juxtaposition of disparate elements in the image.

Imagine There Is a War and No One Is Watching

Joerg Bader

> *In my photographic work I was always especially entranced . . . by the moment when the shadows of reality, so to speak, emerge out of nothing on the exposed paper, as memories do in the middle of the night, darkening again if you try to cling to them, just like a photographic print left in the developing bath too long.*
>
> W. G. Sebald, *Austerlitz*

Peter Piller turned to a war-related topic for the first time in 2003, with the outbreak of the Iraq War, or the Third Gulf War, which was triggered by the world's greatest military power on the basis of lies and fake photographs. Piller's work *Nachkriegsordnung* (Postwar Order) comprises 35 night photographs from the bombing of Baghdad, removed from their context and glued onto German DIN A4 sheets of paper. They are labeled with latitude and longitude coordinates – an allusion to the propaganda of the "clean war" with "pinpoint bomb strikes." In one of the rare cases in which the artist has sourced photographs from a press agency, the color photographs from the German Press Agency (dpa) come from 35 different German daily newspapers and depict the same motif 35 times. *Nachkriegsordnung* makes us aware of the Third Gulf War by revealing the synchronized activation of the mass media, without even a hint as to the newspaper headlines.

The two wars waged by the United States and its allies against Iraq in 1991 and 2003, and the resulting image politics, aroused a new consciousness among artists. Their "discourse" is a "war" against the propaganda of the belligerents, and with nearly the same means of electronic image production as that of the U.S. armed forces. All of Silicon Valley – meaning the entire American computer industry, including Apple – received massive investments at the start of the PC revolution directly from the U.S. Department of War, sorry, Defense.

Bernd Hüppauf articulated the situation brilliantly and provocatively: "No war without discourse." In his book *Was ist Krieg?* (What Is War?), published in 2013, he makes a unique attempt to frame this complex interaction of war, culture, and peace in the context of modernity, that is, the last two hundred years: "There is no war without a social discourse of reflection, imagination, and memory," he writes. “Discourse is at war. At the same time, war is always a discourse.” And further: “War without the discourse of signs and media would not be war; it would not be real. Only discourse makes it real. Encompassing technology, death, and other realities, it is a construct that is an aggregate of thinking, acting, imagining, and cultural interactions.”[1]

Peter Piller found a further war theme through a different context that is still linked to war: aerial photography. The genre was already a source of inspiration for modern art years ago. In his 1927 book *The Non-Objective World*, Kazimir Malevich refers to aerial photographs by military reconnaissance to demonstrate how his notion of Suprematism was the most liberated from the material world. But he is not the only champion of abstraction; El Lissitzky and Piet Mondrian were also enthusiastic about the “abstract” view from above, thanks to this military technology. A late and distant derivative of military aerial reconnaissance is the inventory of around 20 000 aerial photographs of single-family homes that Peter Piller acquired in 2002.

For years, Piller sorted through this mountain of aerial photographs, which can now be found in the *Peter Piller Archive* under the heading *Von Erde schöner* (More Beautiful from Earth). Within this he created 23 enigmatic subcategories, such as *Verbindungsbilder* (Compound Images) or *Projektionsflächen* (Projection Surfaces). Like a needle in a haystack, the artist found a photograph with the shadow of a jet fighter, barely discernable against the woods. In another photo, white-striped street markings, in front of one of the houses, look like a bomb. Today, the *Peter Piller Archive* counts three series depicting bombs or missiles; in total there are seven series that have to do with war and the military.

A year after *Nachkriegsordnung* came a bomb series with a more confusing title. *Unangenehme Nachbarn* (Unpleasant Neighbors) consists of German postcards depicting unexploded bombs and missiles from World War I, which originated mainly from French estuaries, or better, “orifices”: various postcard images are laden with sexual innuendo. Take, for example, the photograph of a young man sitting on a hill, marveling at a meter-high missile that seems to be ascending from between his legs. Clear connotations can also be seen in the photograph of a dud bomb piercing a tree trunk, or when a five- to six-year-old boy with long curls (or is it a girl?) holds his index finger to a much larger bomb standing next to him. An exception to the series, the latter photograph originates from a French source, as indicated by the two lines of French text at the bottom of the picture, reading: *BOMBARDEMENT DE NANCY 13 AOÛT 1916*. Many of the postcards show French or English bombs that missed their goal – perhaps due to poor air reconnaissance. In any case, it was a boon for German propaganda, which was active in the use of postcards.

The series *Unangenehme Nachbarn* prefigures a deliberate downplaying by the artist of the subject matter, as in the case of the boy in *Bombardment of Nancy*, or the humanizing of *Blindgänger-Familie: Eine Sammlung bis zur 28 cm Granate* (Dud Bomb Family: A Collection of Grenades up to 28 cm) from the sub-series *Deko + Munition* (Decoration + Ammunition). The *Blindgänger-Familie* postcard presents an arrangement of several shells, with the smallest in the front and the larger ones in the back – almost like a picture by artists Peter Fischli and David Weiss, and definitely like a family portrait.

For years, without really knowing what to do with them, Peter Piller downloaded eBay photographs of ammunition shells and unexploded bombs. Pictured in kitchens, on dining room chairs, in front of televisions, next to CD racks, in the bedroom in front of a mirrored wardrobe, or simply polished like the living-room parquet floor, perched before the drapes and the radiator – they always appear in a lower-middle-class domestic setting. According to Piller, the market for defused bomb casings flourishes mostly in Germany and France, and especially in Belgium. In this case, "defused" pertains not only to the explosive force of the bomb, but also to the explosive force of the object's significance. There are only a few compact, man-made objects that are as destructive to humanity and the earth's flora and fauna as bombs. And likely no one from the global middle class is unaware that, over the last one hundred years, bombings have left rooms, buildings, entire apartment blocks, districts, and cities in ruins and have taken millions of lives.

Writing chronologically, I now come to the last group of bomb photos: the series *Bombenentschärfer* (Bomb Disposal Technicians) as a subcategory of Peter Piller's collection *Tageszeitungen nach Bildern* (Newspapers after Images). At times, the artist has questioned the category *Bombenentschärfer*, as these bomb disposal technicians are "actually too funny." The pixelated newspaper images show various men, with or without mustaches (many with), who had defused stray bombs shortly before the photograph was taken and were now holding hold them up to the local newspaper photographer for documentation. The underlying humor cannot be denied, for the bomb squads pose with their dirt-crusted missiles like proud fishermen with their biggest catch. Or, as Piller notes, "The bombs are presented like gardeners showing off their prize zucchinis." Despite the chuckle effect of the photographs, I did feel a bit uneasy when viewing these images, and especially when the artist assured me that defusing bombs remains a lucrative business in Germany.

What unites the bomb pictures of the *Peter Piller Archive* is not something pronounced, but something more underlying. The horror of the (bomb) wars is not visible; artists are aware of the pornography of marketing human suffering on capitalist-organized news channels. W. G. Sebald addressed this, writing: "The reproduction of horror, or better: the recreation of horror, be it with images or with letters, is something that is fundamentally problematic. A mass grave cannot be described. This means that one must find other, more tangential ways to do so, accessing memory through archaeology and archives, . . ."[2] Increasingly since the Second Gulf War and even earlier, for example Bertolt Brecht in his *War Primer* or John Heartfield with his photomontages, artists have developed other strategies of war-related image production and distribution that are quite different from those of the war propagators. This is certainly one explanation for the silence surrounding the bomb pictures in the *Peter Piller Archive.* But I suspect that it is not the only one.

The Allies later referred to the interaction of air mines, phosphorous explosives, and incendiary sticks as "Hamburgization." Between 1940 and 1945, 107 000 bombs were dropped on Hamburg and 11 000 unexploded bombs were defused, according to Wikipedia. Around 2 900 have yet to be discovered. For Peter Piller, his series of unexploded bombs is a collection of potential "late bloomers." Figuratively speaking, archives are also potential late bloomers. It thus seems to me that W. G. Sebald's thinking and writing are helpful when considering the *Peter Piller Archive.* Not only because the repressed debate that Sebald sparked coincides temporally with the start of Peter Piller's "militaria," but also because both artists rely on documentary material in an effort to remember. Probably inspired by Walter Benjamin, W. G. Sebald developed a montage technique using descriptions, documents, reflections, photographs, snippets from paintings, and facsimiles of tickets and invoices. Meanwhile, Peter Piller has created an archive that includes drawings, captions, and photographs that are either his own or stem from the photographic management of our daily life.

With the subjective ordering of documents used to develop fictions, Peter Piller, like W. G. Sebald, strives to synthesize our reading of history through narration. In addition, Sebald's preference for mundane photographs from family albums and history and geography books is comparable to Peter Piller's work with photographs from local newspapers and company archives. Both pursue the banality of daily life, knowing that the most unconscious contemporaneity of the past is embedded in these images.

Immer noch Sturm (Still Stormy) is a series of photographic images, very gray and not at all attractive, which only depict landscapes. A surging sea, the barren earth, occasionally tree trunks where all else has burned to the ground. These are images that instantly recall the ravaged German cities, and indeed, the strips of land pictured are the legacy of warriors with their tanks and canons. The similarity between the solid and the liquid landscapes fascinates the artist and they are clearly linked to the "bomb chapter" in his archive. While the waves exude a certain neutrality, the earthen landscapes are "uninhabitable like the moon" – to quote the title of a play staged by Rainer Werner Fassbinder – and not even suitable for the scenery of Samuel Beckett's *Waiting for Godot*, for what audience would want to watch such melancholy for longer than five minutes?

These landscapes of the soul bring to mind an interview with W. G. Sebald, conducted shortly after the publication of *On the Natural History of Destruction*,[3] in which he points out that one could "not address all these things for very long without taking damage, even to one's health." Even if one would merely try "to sketch it," that would actually be "more than one could bear," and it would be impossible "to plumb the depths of the trauma in the souls of those who escaped from the epicenters of catastrophe."[4]

The most recent *Peter Piller Archive* series, *Afghanistan Field Research*, was created in 2014 and is sourced from a botany book on vegetation in Afghanistan. The block of nine photographs is made up of flower portraits. At its center is a photo of an open hand holding crushed blackberries. For the past 35 years, Afghanistan has been a war-torn country: first occupied by the Soviet Union, then shaken by civil war, subjugated by the Taliban, and, since 2001, controlled by an allied coalition of the United States. This is also where the German military was charged by the United Nations mandate "to support the interim Afghan government in establishing and preserving internal security and human rights," as the German Bundeswehr explains on its website.[5] The metaphor that Peter Piller found for a nation that has known only war for an entire generation can be compared to the tactic followed by Jeff Wall for *Dead Troops Talk* (but is achieved the other way around) in its compression of a historical situation.

In this sense, the *Peter Piller Archive* can be understood as a work of art that attempts, with the most rudimentary documentary aesthetics, to create a visual memory of our present time. In the discussions surrounding the importance of documents and of fiction – that happened at the same time as Sebald's debate about the bombings of German cities during World War II – Dieter Forte comes to similar conclusions as Sebald: "We imagine that we can write everything down and hold on to it, in order to pass it on. I feel this is a mistake. If it is not passed through compressed storytelling from generation to generation, so that it makes a deep impression, becoming an unforgettable nightmare vision in the narrative, it will be lost to our descendants."[6]

1 Bernd Hüppauf, *Was ist Krieg*, Transcript, Bielefeld, 2013, p. 32.

2 W. G. Sebald, "Hitlers pyromanische Phantasien," in: Volker Hage (ed.), *Zeugen der Zerstörung: Die Literaten und der Luftkrieg; Essays und Gespräche*, Fischer, Frankfurt am Main, 2003, p. 264.

3 W. G. Sebald, *On the Natural History of Destruction*, trans. Anthea Bell, Modern Library, New York, 2004.

4 W. G. Sebald cited by Volker Hage, "Literaten und der Luftkrieg: 'Es war das eigentlich Nicht-Mögliche,'" in: *Der Spiegel*, July 22, 2003, available online at: www.spiegel.de/kultur/gesellschaft/literaten-und-der-luftkrieg-es-war-das-eigentlich-nicht-moegliche-a-257533.html, accessed 09/02/2014.

5 "Die Internationale Sicherheitsbeistands-Truppe ISAF (International Security Assistance Force), deren Aufstellung der Weltsicherheitsrat am 20. Dezember 2001 beschloss, soll im Auftrag der Vereinten Nationen die afghanische Interimsregierung bei der Wahrung der Menschenrechte sowie bei der Herstellung und Wahrung der inneren Sicherheit unterstützen," available online at: www.kmba.militaerseelsorge.bundeswehr.de/portal/a/kmba/!ut/p/c4/Hca7DYAwDAXAWVjA7unYAmjQC59gxXEQDrA-CF1zPPLHcEtElWJQ7nmYpQ0PZVFfV_Up5QD6W85luFxhixO2uMPEK4yP1DUvqqiKVA!!/, accessed 09/02/2014.

6 Dieter Forte, "Menschen werden zu Herdentieren," in: *Der Spiegel*, April 5, 1999, available online at: www.spiegel.de/spiegel/print/d-10933003.html, accessed 09/02/2014.

Breaking Ground, for Example

Elisabetta Antonelli

It was my first job, and my heart was pounding as I hung up the telephone after what had turned out to be an unpleasant conversation. The manuscript I requested did not exist. And he had issues with those in my profession anyway, he said on the other end of the line. The profession to which I was aspiring was anything but a picnic. I sensed it immediately.

That was almost exactly fifteen years ago. I had just begun an internship at the Winterthur *Landbote* newspaper. Having spent my childhood and youth in Zurich's Weinland region, I was sent to Benken for the August 1 festivities on Swiss National Day. Gerhard Blocher was speaking there, the older brother of the infamous Christoph Blocher, the Swiss People's Party (SVP) *Nationalrat* (Federal Councillor) at the time. I was to call Gerhard Blocher, the former pastor and local council leader of Hallau back then to request the manuscript of his speech, as it would help me with my article. But with the very first phone call that I would make as a local journalist, I had already run into trouble.

It was my first practical lesson: proximity is often a greater challenge than distance. There is nothing easier than criticizing Barack Obama and printing an unfavorable picture of him in the local newspaper; he will not complain. But beware: depict a municipal councillor in the wrong light, and both amicability and access will be promptly terminated.

Despite the brush-off on the phone by the former Pastor Blocher, I went resolutely and unprepared to Benken and took my notes. He had spoken about "the job that had to be done." The resulting article appeared alongside many other reports on the national holiday, during which famous and less famous guest speakers mused about the country. The articles covering their speeches on "freedom," "reflection," and "national treasures" were accompanied by a single photograph: the traditional August 1 bonfire, a subject we all know so well.

No Scandal Here

There is no national newspaper that would address such topics. There is no scoop and no scandal. August 1 falls under the category: events at our doorstep and tradition.

What does happen at our doorstep is the *raison d'être* of the local newspaper. Today one speaks of USP – short for "unique selling proposition/point." In local journalism this means: no one else reports on this topical and local subject, neither the competition (which usually does not even exist), nor the news agencies.

August 1 is only one of many recurring events that a municipal newspaper reports on. There is also the *Albanifest* (St. Alban's Festival), the *Fasnachtsböögg* (Burning of the Winter Bogey), the *Frackwoche* (Tailcoat Week), and *Afro-Pfingsten* (an African music festival). Events for locals in the know. We also cover the ARA (municipal wastewater treatment system), the local guild (e.g., for the fire department), the city roundabout, the expansion of the school building, and so on. Topics from daily life that we all know and must remain informed about, if we are interested in what happens at our doorstep.

The local newspapers, which can be purchased at the newsstands for a few francs, do this at a fairly good journalistic level. Not only in words, but also in pictures, of course – the days of dense text are gone for good. Today, the general rule is: no text without a picture. The feud between writers and graphic designers has been over since the turn of the millennium. There is no more debate about text over image or vice versa. It is a given that the readership's interest must be won together with the image and the presentation. According to *The New Journalism Handbook* by Wolf Schneider and Paul-Josef Raue, published in 2012 by Rowohlt in Berlin, "a picture is, in contrast to a text, not better nor worse information: it describes something differently than a text. It requires interpretation, it invokes emotion – and it encourages one to learn more about the background of the moment in which the photographer pressed the shutter release."

That is certainly the ideal case: the local journalist is in the midst of the action and takes the photograph at the most important moment. However, we do not always find that action. Instead, we report once a year about the August 1 celebration. How can you illustrate that without being boring? Therein lies the art.

The One Thing That Press Photos Must Not Do

Andrea Fessler from Winterthur is a photo editor and graphic designer. A long-time employee of the photo agency Prisma, she has been part of the *Landbote* editorial staff for eight years. Every day she views hundreds of photographs. Her mission is to make photography come alive for the newspaper. To do so, she pays attention to general criteria such as motif, composition, crop, and placement – it's part of her craft. Yet for her, the perfect picture must do even more: "A good press photo should inform, address, agitate, animate, attract, surprise, enlighten, question, and validate. There is only one thing it must not do: bore."

But for local newspapers there are pitfalls everywhere: for example, when there is no one standing at the pedestrian zone that must be photographed. Or when the employees of the local butchery, which is celebrating its anniversary, are all grouped behind the counter with a friendly smile. Or at an annual event. It's been seen a hundred times.

What Somewhat Concerns Us

Peter Piller makes use of this danger zone. He culls images and recombines them in his own categories. The August 1 celebration would most likely find a place in his section *Mensch und Feuer* (Man and Fire). Tomato plants ripped out of the garden would certainly belong to the *Vandalismus* (Vandalism) series. A gardener standing next to them with slouched shoulders suggestive of this misfortune would surely be categorized as *Vandalismus zeigen* (Showing Vandalism). Peter Piller's categories often cause us to laugh, because they reframe that which occurs at our doorstep. For example, *Tanz vor Logo* (Dancing in Front of the Logo). We know that one as well. The Turnerchränzli (annual town acrobatics performance) in Dättlikon comes immediately to mind.

And yet, Piller does not ridicule the themes and photographs from the local newspaper. Instead, he makes us aware of what surrounds us every day and what we are interested in, or at least what should interest us. After all, the construction of a retirement home financed by our taxes begins with the breaking of the ground. And it is this breaking of the ground at our doorstep that somewhat concerns us.

But we also feel caught in the act, because we have not recognized the categories as such. And because Piller with his work shows us what our lives are made of and what is happening around us. Sometimes it is not at all exciting, but provincial and tacky. And we don't necessarily want to accept that.

Local journalism with its depiction of local stories is not all that bad. Because what is close to us can also be amazingly exotic. Does Piller know about the Müllcontainer Grand Prix in Oberembrach, where racecars are crafted from trash bins? Or the Holidi at Graben in Winterthur, the nude wooden statue (locally referred to as the *Pimmelmann*, or "penis man"), its days no longer numbered thanks to a local initiative? Piller has yet to create the categories for photos such as these.

The August 1 pictures are indeed similar. They will appear in the newspaper again this year, and the year after as well. Just like when I had to deliver my first journalistic work. But it doesn't matter, really. For when the 100th Veltemer Dorfest (village festival) comes around, we will still want to see the children eating their cotton candy. And the Ferris wheel at the Albanifest. The Fasnachtsböögg and the Guggenmusik (carnival marching band). Not to mention the August 1 bonfire.

Note on Banality
For Peter Piller

Marcus Steinweg

1. Self-Transcendence

Nietzsche speaks of the overcoming of the self, while Heidegger chooses the formula "self-overreaching as self-grasping"[1] to mark the transcendental character of the subject or of being.[2] With this designation, the terms human, self-consciousness, I, and reason all lose their substantiality. It is about the definition of the subject as a hyperbolic being or animal with a talent for excess. That the animal in Heidegger's dispositive remains stunned and strung into its environment, instead of a world only having an environment and a circumference,[3] means that it is incapable of excess. Man, however, the *animal rationale* or *zoon logon echon*, is capable of unreason, as long as unreason means the transgression of reason, the disruption of the *logos* and transgression of economy. Precisely this is what makes man into a subject: the capacity to be something other than an object (of the circumstances, of time, its culture and language). The subject is already a subject of self-transcendence qua subject. It reaches out beyond itself. This turns it into a feverish vector toward the uncertain, which ascribes itself to the indefinite of the future as an incommensurable contingency.[4] It opens itself to its ontological indeterminacy and disquiet. Even if one was tempted to view this disquiet skeptically (there are a thousand reasons to do so), or if one caught a glimpse of the index of one's freedom and chance to self-seizure, what seems unquestionable is that what we call the human subject is everything but a cogito articulating itself on stable grounds. Jean-Luc Nancy is right when he says that we have begun to think "a disturbance referring to that which is actually 'reason'"[5] (since Descartes, since Kant, with Nietzsche, Freud, and Lacan).[6]

Reason borders on unreason, the subject grazes its abyss, of which it can neither be said that it belongs to it, nor that it is external. Its situation is this complex, this contradictory, this disquieting.

The philosophy of the twentieth century has manifested itself in diverse forms as the detection and examination of this abyss, in order to stand up to the double task of the delimitation of rationalistic hubris on the one hand, and resistance to the temptation of irrationalism on the other. We have to grasp the abyss and the abyss of freedom, like Schelling, Heidegger, and Sartre did. The experience of freedom becomes the experience of a certain horror, the void and desert, in which the subject perceives itself to be faced with the death of God. As *horror vacui*, this horror is the horror of the absence of a given and final meaning. Just like Nietzsche's *madman* in section 125 of *The Gay Science*, the subject suffers its world as unchained from the sun and tumbling and falling in all directions:

> What were we doing when we unchained this earth from its sun? Where is it moving to now? Where are we moving to? Away from all suns? Are we not continually falling? And backwards, sidewards, forwards, in all directions? Is there still an up and a down? Aren't we straying as though through an infinite nothing? Isn't empty space breathing at us? Hasn't it got colder? Isn't night and more night coming again and again? . . . God is dead! God remains dead! And we have killed him![7]

With the unchaining of the earth from the sun and the death of God, the subject experiences the instability of reality as the inconsistency of its world. The experience of the abyss becomes the experience of an elementary disorientation and freedom, which implies a certain "suspension of the Ground."[8] It is the experience of ontological incommensurability, which reveals all the commensurabilities of the subject – all its certainties, values, evidences, and consistencies – as the abysmal qualities they are.

Viewed in an existentialist light, the subject finds itself confronted with the Nothing, which is yet another index of its desertion and solitude.[9] There is no guarantor for sense, meaning, or value. There is nothing but the growing desert: the indifference of the Cosmos toward Man, which today is addressed by the protagonists of Speculative Realism and Object-oriented Philosophy.[10] The Cosmos is acosmic. Instead of representing a meaningful order, it bursts in accelerating expansion into nowhere. One would have to speak of the *ontological distraction* of the totality of being. Nothing indicates that it is subject to an ultimate principle.[11] Wittgenstein has gazed upon the mystical of the world not in terms of *how* but *that* it is: "It's not *how* things are in the world that is mystical, but *that* it exists."[12]

The "miracle of the existence of the world"[13] indicates its contingency and inexplicability. However, contingency and inexplicability do not apply to *how* the world is (its immanence); they apply solely to their naked *that* (its implicit transcendence).

2. Rift in Immanence

There is no transcendence, provided the word refers to a beyond or a meta-world. Yet the phantasm of the beyond cannot be substituted by a phantasm of the here and now. This is Nietzsche's elementary lesson; it presents us with the task of thinking the infinite under the conditions of finiteness, freedom under the conditions of lack of freedom, transcendence under the conditions of immanence, which is by no means a relapse into the religious. Sure, there is nothing but immanence! But, as Frédéric Neyrat formulates in reference to Jean-Luc Nancy, it is a *torn immanence*.[14]

The rift in immanence opens up immanence in itself. It keeps it open and inhibits its closure. This does not mean that the world of immanence (the here and now, the constituting reality, the shared world, the homogeneous space of facts) opens itself toward a second world of transcendence (the beyond). We are not dealing with a two-world ontotheology – like classical Metaphysics was. Instead of opening toward opening, it is about an opening toward closure:

> ... for the world is the gulf that swallows every type of backworld. The world is strangeness itself, absolute strangeness: the strangeness of the real, the quite tangible reality of this anomaly or of this exception devoid of all attachment.[15]

The passage leading to a second World is blocked by the factum of its inexistence. That God is dead means that this secondary World does not exist. Yet there is a door. Only this door does not open to the outside. It opens to the inside. It opens immanence toward its implicit transcendence. Naturally, this is not the old (religious, theological) transcendence. It's not something given, not a positive entity whatsoever. It is an immanent transcendence, which indicates nothing but the ontological inconsistency or non-closedness of the texture of immanence. In conversation with Daniel Tyradellis, Nancy elaborates:

> When I say immanence, you will immediately ask if it's the immanence of Deleuze. No, not in the sense of Deleuze. Let's put it this way: this pure being-in-itself und remaining-in-itself, the in-itself – Hegel's, if you will – so this in-itself by Hegel is rigid, mute, dumb and does not initiate anything. Something only begins if an it, if there is such a thing, escapes itself and becomes an in-and-of-itself, etc. Yet under wisdom and knowledge we always understand something like a final state, a (finite?) situation in which we don't need or want anything anymore, and don't even desire anything anymore. And Deleuze, who positions himself in a similar way against lust as the end of

desire, thinks lust, just like wisdom or knowledge, as a state in which there is nothing left to desire. But what does that mean? Maybe, firstly, thinking mostly means desiring. And to desire means, I'd say, to orient oneself according to something, to let something stress you.[16]

Desire (*désir*) transposes thinking and guarantees its tension. It overstretches thinking toward the inconsistency of the consistency texture of *immanence*, *world*, or *reality*, which I have called *transcendence*. The texture of immanence is not an immanently calm zone. Its promise of calmness indicates the abyss of perpetual turbulence *ex negativo*. This turbulence does not only apply to the subject. It applies to the entire fabric of the World, the acosmic Cosmos accelerating and moving toward the indefinite. Now it is all about fathoming how thinking can relate to this disturbance.

Certainly not by reducing, neutralizing, or ignoring it. Rather, it affirms its being contaminated by it, in order to constitute itself as a thinking of disturbance in a double sense. As the restless thinking of restlessness. As the tense touch of the points of inconsistency of its world. The rift or rifts in immanence mark the constituting fragility of the texture of reality. Just like the subject, it lacks ultimate consistency.

3. Banality

I propose to call *banality* that which indicates the character of indifference, contingency, and inconsistency of our world. Instead of giving in to the temptation of dramatizing the described events, the – albeit breathless – thinking of the ontological disturbance of acosmic being implies a kind of quiet affirmation. It is already Nietzsche who, with his *amor fati* and the idea of the eternal return of the same, calls for such affirmation. While still dramatic in its tone, the Nietzschean affirmation ultimately demands the de-dramatization of the subject and its world. The World is the whole that withdraws itself. Totality of being at the limit of being. Something protruding from the Nothing, the banal manifestations or elements of which already indicate the absence of a closed totality. The World is the index of some kind of ontological banality, which is why being in the world means to be poised above the Nothing, to lend a face to that which gives it away. World could be called the dynamic union of Chaos and Cosmos, the chaosmotic Universe (one wouldn't be far from Joyce or Deleuze and Guattari). One could also say that the World expresses, or rather *articulates*, a clamping of transcendence and immanence. World, then, would be the mostly witnessless, sometimes witnessed, described and marveled at articulation of positively indifferent and anonymous and, in this sense, banal world affairs. Articulation of the totality of being as the development of its cracking and discontinuity. Hence the word *world* denominates the excess both of the term and of thinking. The thinking which opens toward the World has long been opened by it, though not gently and forgiving, but relentlessly and permanent. The World has long dug itself into our thinking. It explodes over and over again in the heart of the subject. This is how banal our situation is.

1 Martin Heidegger, *Schelling's Treatise on the Essence of Human Freedom (1809)*, trans. Joan Stambaugh, Ohio University Press, Athens, 1985.

2 Let us remember that Heidegger already talks about the "transcendental character of being" in: *Being and Time*, trans. Joan Stambaugh, State University of New York Press, Albany, 1996. The problem of transcendence is furthermore discussed in depth in: *The Metaphysical Foundations of Logic*, trans. Michael Heim, Indiana University Press, Indianapolis, 1992.

3 See Martin Heidegger, *The Fundamental Concepts of Metaphysics: World, Finitude, Solitude*, trans. William McNeill and Nicholas Walker, Indiana University Press, Indianapolis, 1995, pp. 42ff.

4 Karl Jaspers has rightly insisted that the vector of overcoming remains obscure in Nietzsche: "the last word is never and nowhere spoken by him." Quotations from the German and French sources cited in this essay have been translated by Paul Feigelfeld. See also Karl Jaspers, *Nietzsche and Christianity*, 2nd ed., Henry Regnery, Chicago, 1963.

5 Jean-Luc Nancy and Daniel Tyradellis, *Was heißt uns Denken?*, diaphanes, Zurich and Berlin, 2013, p. 74.

6 Blanchot speaks of the "eternal unrest" of a subject, which "remains excluded from the promised land of truth." See Maurice Blanchot, *The Sirens' Song: Selected Essays*, Indiana University Press, Bloomington, 1982.

7 Friedrich Nietzsche, *The Gay Science*, trans. Josefine Nauckhoff, Cambridge University Press, Cambridge, 2001, p. 120. Peter Sloterdijk comments on this passage by insisting that "the *pro forma* equally arranged variants of falling 'backward,' 'sideward,' 'in all directions' are but epiphenomena of the main vector of the fall 'forward.' 'Forward' means: away from the old 'center of security,' away from all that was formerly state, measure, and good reason. If fall and precipitancy [*Sturz und Überstürzung*] are one, then God is dead in the vehicles of this motion." See Peter Sloterdijk, *Die schrecklichen Kinder der Neuzeit: Über das anti-genealogische Experiment der Moderne*, Suhrkamp, Berlin, 2014, p. 72. On precipitancy as the fundamental motion of the subject, see Marcus Steinweg, *Philosophie der Überstürzung*, Merve Verlag, Berlin, 2013.

8 Slavoj Žižek, *The Indivisible Remainder: On Schelling and Related Matters*, Verso Books, London, 2007, p. 20.

9 Heidegger has distinguished between the *Seinsverlassenheit des Seins* (abandonment by being of Being) and the *Seinsvergessenheit des (menschlichen) Daseins* (oblivion by being of human existence). See Martin Heidegger, *Contributions to Philosophy (of the Event)*, trans. Richard Rojcewicz and Daniela Vallega-Neu, Indiana University Press, Indianapolis, 2012.

10 These positions are connected by the attempt to include "the moment of horror into its thinking." See Armen Avanessian and Björn Quiring (eds.), *Abyssus Intellectualis*, Merve Verlag, Berlin, 2013, p. 12.

11 Quentin Meillassoux writes: "... if nothing exists beyond the laws of the world, to rule the world, then because these laws do not exist, that they do not govern the future (*devenir*), but are themselves governed by a becoming (*devenir*) without law, so that they have no reason to last forever." See Quentin Meillassoux, "L'inexistence divine," in: Alexandre Costanzo and Daniel Costanzo (eds.), *Failles N°3: Existence / Inexistence*, Paris, 2014, pp. 55–60, esp. p. 55.

12 Ludwig Wittgenstein, *Tractatus logico-philosophicus*, trans. D. F. Pears and B. F. McGuinness, Routledge Classics, London and New York, 2001, Sect. 6.44, p. 88.

13 Ludwig Wittgenstein, "A Lecture on Ethics" (1929), cited from: www.geocities.jp/mickindex/wittgenstein/witt_lec_et_en.html, accessed 09/15/2014.

14 Frédéric Neyrat, "Jean-Luc Nancy: An Existential Communism," in: *Parrhesia*, vol. 17, 2013, pp. 25–28.

15 Jean-Luc Nancy, *Adoration: The Deconstruction of Christianity II*, trans. John McKeane, Fordham University Press, New York, 2013, p. 33.

16 Nancy, Tyradellis, op. cit.

when the early morning mist has lifted

Peter Piller

my heart is occupied elsewhere

i was as unaware then as i am now why it was that i, as a young boy from the hunsrück area, mapped the nests of buzzards and falcons in the surrounding woodlands and collected their feathers and even pellets.

my little ornithological library and collections were lost in various house moves later, and my enthusiasm for birds naturally waned with my growing interest in the borussia mönchengladbach football team, the girl from leipzig in the next class, and a band called trio from the town of großenkneten.

but interests that are sidelined or overshadowed as the hormones kick in do not die out; they remain, encapsulated, going unnoticed for decades until they suddenly reemerge. In the new milennium, pushed further along the track of life, they naturally called promptly for access to photography, which initially only meant going an additional 300 mm to the existing camera.

but what i regarded at first as a harmless pastime and an artless space ultimately evolved, within just two years, into a technical and emotional arms race with myself. i would love to know how it came about that i have ended up spending three-quarters of my free time photographing birds, and lost to the world.

picture perfect

lenses with greater focal lengths and increased light intensity have made binoculars unecessary in identifying birds. 12 800 iso renders just about anything visible – and can it still be called photography when it is so far removed from what the eye can see? am i observing the birds or am i watching them?

whereas at first the delight of actually spotting some particular species was all that was needed – along with a photo as evidence, a tiny black silhouette in the middle of the picture – better lens quality brought out the detailed outlines of individual feathers and the gleam in the eye of a bird in flight.

some of my shots could grace a double-page spread in *geo* magazine, surpassing by far the quality of analogue photographs in old-fashioned reference books, in which the photographers occasionally cheated by staging stuffed birds in a natural setting.

having arrived at such a picture-perfect point, i could easily have spent the next decade photographing every possible species in summer and winter plumage, perched and in flight, or better still in mating flight, with their young, with their food and so on, had it not been for a nagging sense of disappointment amidst all this professionality. it was not just the sheer obscenity of my photographic equipment that had already long since made me take "the path less traveled," but the photos themselves with their scalpel-sharp quality that i basically cannot not bear to see. the bird photographed as though in isolation had so little in common with the actual experience of the moment that there were days when i would cart my ten or so kilos of equipment around as usual, but my pleasure in photography had dwindled to the point that the very words "i'm going to take some pictures" no longer rang true.[1]

waiting or the eternal recurrence of the same

so perhaps instead of going to take pictures, i went to wait.[2]

and going to wait is harder than one might think; it is an active state rather than a passive one. keeping myself and the camera constantly at the ready in preparation for a moment that might not come again so soon, while at the same time keeping an eye on the constantly changing light conditions, applying local knowledge to anticipate possible directions of flight, determining birdcalls and signs, reading traces, all demand the same kind of attentiveness as angling, albeit with the difference that in angling – in which respect that murderous pastime is even more amazing! – it is mostly about anticipating what is going on unseen below the surface of the water. in both instances, though, it is often chance that directs the decisive moment.[3]

it took a while before i realized that it wasn't my three-volume ornithological guide to germany's best birdwatching sites that was the problem, but that i had to revisit these places multiple times if i wanted to spot anything more interesting than a house sparrow.[4]

the mistakes

photographing a bird in flight is a challenge, if only because directing a focal length of 1000 mm at a tiny sliver of sky makes it so difficult to get the bird in the viewfinder quickly. once that does happen, continuous shooting can capture small narratives and motion studies but often ends up with parts missing, birds without claws, headless birds, cropped wings, or cut-off primary feathers. sometimes all that can be seen at the edge of the picture might be some tail feathers or even no bird at all, or even a telegraph mast in sharp focus with a blurry falcon diving swiftly to the ground behind it.

it's incredible how many of these documentations of my failed efforts i had to delete before actually realizing the potential of these images![5]

the spanish imperial eagle

annoying as it may be to find that the wings of a house sparrow have been cropped in an image, this same flaw is gladly accepted after spending half the day waiting to spot a spanish imperial eagle. but are these huge and magnificent birds really the ones i am looking for, or should i perhaps concentrate more on the most common of all birds, such as the blackbird perched on every fence, mimicking the latest tv theme tune, or the common buzzard lurking by the highway waiting for roadkill, in all their different plumage from near-white to variegated shades to the darkest brown, or should i even search for an avian alter ego to accompany and study?[6]

the out-takes

for the most part, it seems that nothing happens for a long time.

nevertheless,[7] in a state of tense expectation, without music and most certainly without a smartphone, where – if not here and now – could there be the opportunity of quietly observing the growth of the trees, the breeze among the branches, the scudding clouds, the incoming mist of the evening, the build of the mecklenburg raised hides, or the clouds rising behind the tractors – all of which means activating a way of seeing that is free of any use value?[8]

now, in the last few months, i have started photographing the car waiting for me in its woodland solitude – a dark gray body of metal skeptically enclosed by green foliage, and the perches of game birds on which, unfortunately, none are perching, and more generally the habitats as well as my own traces that i leave behind in the hides or on the grass. And sometimes i take note of the few occasional dialogues: "i am the gamekeeper here; i am about to commence the hunt and therefore . . ." (with a strong accent on at least every other syllable). "ok, i'm leaving."[9]

when i got back from my vacation last week and went to switch on my computer, my operating system showed an error that read along the lines of "mac applications dxyzz7++kmd, gpeut5 lls" or something similar and, after a few cold starts, phone calls, restoring the system to a couple of weeks back, and an entire morning spent at the local mac premium support center, it was repaired, but the photos i had taken on vacation were all lost. the hobby in flight with a dragonfly in its beak; the almost-white buzzard, which was either blind or so besotted that it did not try to flee but instead stayed photogentically in place for a couple of minutes against the dark forest backdrop, even though i was just five yards away in my car; the great grey shrike hovering in the air; the white-tailed eagle against the sun, its every feather detailed by the light; the osprey emerging from the water and flying away with a carp in its beak. all gone. irrevocably. never to return. but that is not so bad, really, for it is only the photographic data that is lost. the most important thing is that everything of importance is still there.

1 doubts and crises in the course of the artistic process should, fundamentally, be welcomed. they are signs of still being alive. the mere ability to act in open contradiction of previous statements has to be aimed for.

2 even my studio is, first and foremost, a waiting room. i have never considered the days i have spent waiting to have been wasted, for mostly it was about giving something the time it needed. in order to cope with it all, "waiting activities" such as scanning can be very helpful: you immerse yourself in the seemingly repetitive sounds of the scanner, automatically carry out a few routine tasks, and trust your own mind, or rather your senses, which work in their quiet way, unhampered by thought. what seems to occur quite casually can still be brought into form by thought soon enough. i have never consciously devised any of my works.

3 and it is by no means the worst director. so much can be gained from chance, error, and misunderstanding! only the constant fear of making a mistake is actually unproductive.

4 in dealing with photographic finds of every kind, i have managed, as best i can, to develop patience. the first glance is not to be trusted at all: it's enough to have a vague feeling that "there might be something here." that is worth far more than a stack of images after the first viewing or even an idea of what to do with them. just as every word is surrounded by thousands of associated ideas, so too it is with pictures, only even more so. it is imperative to return, preferably as a different person each time.

5 to store everything has long been one of my guiding principles. in working with archives, it sometimes took years for me to become aware of the potential of individual images that elude any instant legibility.

6 whether you have to let the years pass by, imprisoned in an office, or whether you work artistically – everything, of course, always revolves around everyday routine, which is in itself the goal. and everything that is essential to a solution is already there, on the doorstep, unnoticed and overlooked.

7 yes, it was and still is a goal to do something of which you cannot tell in advance whether it will actually achieve a result or whether it will be deemed in retrospect a complete waste of time. it can only ever be done in defiance of the odds; in praise of defiance.

8 sometimes i start photographing something and have already taken lots of shots, delighting in the sound of the shutter with no thought for art or even for myself as an artist. in those serendipitous moments the work ripples out from the center to the edges, rather than vice versa, and takes hardly any effort because only a few things have to be removed and sorted.

9 often, works have emerged out of previous works, through a momentary break, a change of place, or through unconsciously seeking out an adjacent setting.

Constellation and Critical Mass

An Inevitably Insufficient Typology of the Archival
Between Art and Garbage

Jörg Heiser

Created Truth

Around 1925, much of the philosophical enquiry into rationalism, technicism, and capitalism that was to mark the twentieth century – to sum up the central thesis of Martin Mittelmeier's book *Adorno in Neapel* (2013)[1] – took a decisive turn on the shores of the Gulf of Naples. It was in this place – a romantic focus of longing in the intellectual history of (not only) Germany – that Walter Benjamin met the Latvian theater director and Bolshevik activist Asja Lācis. With her, he devised the concept of *porosity*, as embodied by Naples, and which, in turn, also significantly influenced Alfred Sohn-Rethel, Siegfried Kracauer, and Theodor W. Adorno, all of whom also spent some time in Naples during that period. It is not just the tufa stones of Naples that are porous, but also the way in which the city has been restructured through the centuries, on top of its ruins, wells, and catacombs. The principle of porosity in nature becomes a principle of architecture, life, and thought. Benjamin and Lācis describe it as follows: "The stamp of the definitive is avoided. No situation appears intended forever, no figure asserts it 'thus and not otherwise.'"[2]

Mittelmeier outlines how this "porosity" becomes Adorno's concept of "constellation" – a three-dimensional notion in which seemingly incompatible terms and ideas are circumscribed and reveal themselves as cohesively interconnected only within the overall motivity of the text. This corresponds to Adorno's aim of activating thought in an artistic, unsystematic way, while not allowing it to descend from the systematically analytical into the merely mimetic.

It is the *spatiality* of concepts such as porosity and constellation that is key to understanding the artistic process of the archival. The fact that porosity has connotations of brittleness while constellation has an undertone of pseudoscience (after all, the term comes from astrology) is a necessary and accepted risk. Artistic thinking has to be open to seemingly incidental, illegitimate, and indeed porous knowledge, and even to drawing its initial energy from this. In the early eighteenth century, the Neapolitan philosopher Giambattista Vico formulated his *verum factum* principle – "the true is the made." Just as only God knows the truth about his creation, so, too, do we ourselves bear responsibility for the truths we assert, because the object of our contemplation is in part shaped, and created, by the manner of our contemplation.

A typology of the archival in twentieth- and twenty-first-century art can be outlined with a broad range of aspects in mind: from early cultic and religious writings to the land registers and files used by administrative and (in)justice systems, to libraries and evidence rooms, museum depots and photographic collections, and to the seemingly boundless ocean of digital data; but also from the epistemological paradigms and discourses that can be regarded (in the sense of, say, Foucault) as a living archive – reaching far beyond the accepted concept of physical place. These aspects feature a variety of more or less porous constellations of created truth.

Atlas: Warburg

There is no way around Aby Warburg's *Mnemosyne Atlas* (1924–1929). Even his own private library of 60 000 volumes – funded by his brother Max in exchange for the fact that Aby forfeited to him the right to take over the family banking business – reflects his affinity for artistic ideas. Instead of organizing the books and accompanying collection of some 350 000 photographs according to the usual criteria of epoch, medium, style, et cetera, Aby Warburg archived them according to "elective affinities" and iconological concepts (such as "magic and science"). They do not follow a linear sequence of time or genealogy but form constellations of similarity and contrast. This made it possible to bring back to light even seemingly obscure works that would otherwise have been overshadowed by the great icons and names of the established canon.

The *Mnemosyne Atlas* – 79 wooden panels covered in black cloth on which Warburg arranged constellations of pictures from his archive – was set up in front of the library shelves while he was working on it. The constellations of pictures, which he hoped would provide insight into the legacy of ancient mythology in a "pathos formula" of poses and forms enduring right through to present-day photography, emerged to some extent directly from his reading. They wrested themselves like phantasmagoria from the pages as Warburg read them.

For instance, Warburg arranged cosmological maps around the image of a zeppelin, as though our hopes and fears about a technicalized future were truly written in the heavens. This highly charged form of evocative allegory is as much a reflection of perspectives as it is a shaping of them in the first place. In that respect, it resembles art. But that should not belie the differences between them.

Following Benjamin H.D. Buchloh, it may be asked just how productive it is to compare Warburg's *Atlas* with the collage and photomontage techniques of artists in the 1920s (or the 1960s).[3] Whereas Warburg sought the continuing effect of ancient mythological enchantment in the seemingly profane objects of the present – an idealistic reconstruction of continuities – many avant-garde collage/montage artists sought a distinct break with the past. And whereas Warburg pursued the critical mass of accumulated images (albeit heightened by way of example in each of the 79 panels), the collage/montage – whether by John Heartfield or Hannah Höch – was about singling out individual aspects in deliberate confrontation. In the latter case, archival order plays, at most, a subordinate role: it is not so much about reconstructing cultural memory than about giving voice to the unspoken aspects of the present. This does not, in any way, contradict our current feverish search in the archives of the past, channeling Freud through Derrida, for that which has as yet remained unspoken.[4] It is a search that has long been nurtured by our experience of new ways of seeing, established by the classical avant-garde.

The present, however, is also informed by another shift that occurred in the 1960s: namely, a shift from the *symbolic* constellation to a constellation based on the experience of industrial reproduction and consumption which registers the quiddity of the world in a way that is profanely anti-symbolic and anti-didactic.

Series/Grids: Repetition and Difference

The groundbreaking project by Bernd and Hilla Becher might therefore be described as cartography and, with that, as a form of atlas – were it not determined by an order of alignment and seriality that actually eliminates the cartographical element again. What is being surveyed here is not the seemingly incompatible but the evidently similar. The couple first met in 1957 at the Düsseldorf advertising agency Troost, which was a major player in the market at the time, creating print adverts for brands such as Persil washing powder and the soft drink Sinalco and also designing corporate logos. An appreciation for repetition, alignment, and format may well have been honed there. In the same year, Bernd Becher took some 35 mm photographs of the steelworks earmarked for demolition in his hometown of Siegen – though at the time he did so with the intention of using the photos as an aid to painting. However, unlike Albert Renger-Patzsch who in his groundbreaking 1928 book *Die Welt ist schön* (The World Is Beautiful) explored the world like some strange planet, encyclopedically and reducing it to surface detail, the Bechers pursued a thematic focus based on seriality: photographic series of half-timbered houses stoically scrutinized and always shot in similar conditions, followed soon afterward by a series of industrial architecture.

Ed Ruscha's *Thirtyfour Parking Lots*, published in 1967 as an artist's book, comprises aerial views of mostly empty parking lots in Los Angeles, which seem to follow similar laws of uniformity and industrial banality. Ruscha however, in contrast to the Bechers, was not seeking to document something that was disappearing but to see the everyday, through alien eyes as it were, as something special. What they do have in common is that they regarded something seemingly mundane as worthy of portrayal.

The Bechers' oeuvre is exemplary of a *preserving and yet at the same time new* systematic ordering of found and fabricated artifacts (in this instance existing buildings and their photographic representation). But this definition tells us nothing about the criteria of selection and presentation. Those, in the case of the Bechers, are informed by a positively forensic archival accuracy that accords each object photographed, as far as possible, the same conditions of light and perspective, as well as framing and hanging – not in order to emphasize similarity through repetition, but in order to accentuate differences.

Atlas/Grid: World Filter, Model, Fiction

Starting in the 1960s, Gerhard Richter famously turned the archive of his photographs and found images into an *Atlas* that was an artwork in its own right. Whether it is an *Atlas* in the spirit of Aby Warburg remains to be seen. In Richter's case, it is a kind of collecting point for his own photographs and sketches, but also for the flotsam and jetsam of the media, somewhere "between art and garbage" (Richter), partly charged with the emotionality of intimate family albums, partly taking the disinterested approach of a picture-processing plant. Many artists create cartoons, albums, files, or pinboards. But Richter goes one step further by composing panels on which photos and found images are arranged on sheets according to categories such as similarity/transformation and contrast/reversion, yet at the same time, on another level, quite simply in the sequence in which they came into his hands. Initially, in the mid-1960s, he still followed a principle of loose, mosaic-like arrangements of internal relationships, formally akin to Warburg's work. Already, we find here that the focus is not primarily on associating the disparate, but on the actual sequence, and the recurrence of the mundane alongside the historically significant: newspaper clippings, pictures of his own friends, partners, and family members, toilet paper and chandeliers, soft porn, concentration camps, abstract color samples, gentle landscapes, sunsets, artists' portraits, views of exhibitions, and so forth. There is hardly anything that does not have a place in the *Atlas*. We do not regard this sequence as a series of autonomous images, but as the key and source code to the oeuvre of a true maverick. At the same time, Richter's *Atlas* is also, conversely, a filter for the world, combing through all that is happening half systematically and half intuitively, like the cultural and opinion pages of a newspaper. Warburg also built a filter for the world – a machine for the reconstruction of cultural memory. But with Richter, there is also the criteria of painterly transformability and self-referentiality – which also applies *ex negativo*, when a photo in the *Atlas* is *not* actually used as a model.

Another important factor is that authorship is delegated through the conceptual rules of archiving. The work, in part, writes itself. This is particularly evident in Susan Hiller's *Dedicated to the Unknown Artists* (1972–1976) – a work consisting of fourteen large panels on which more than three hundred postcards of rough seas around the British coast are arranged in grids. The title refers to the unknown photographers and colorists who created these images. The critical mass of postcards shows the rough sea as an expression of British humor regarding poor holiday weather. Hiller has dedicated the painstaking attention of a systematic and anthropologically trained Conceptual artist to this commonplace phenomenon.

Walid Raad goes two steps further with *The Atlas Group*: firstly, by making the work the product of a fictitious collective (founded in 1999) building up an archive (The Atlas Group Archive), and secondly, by making that archive out of fictitious documentation closely based on the recent history of civil-war-torn Lebanon. His approach appears to owe much to literature and film: the gaps created by the psychological repression of memory or physical loss have to be bridged by fiction and are speculatively given a voice. The resulting archival installations feature patterns of series and grids which, though redolent of the work of Becher, Richter, and Hiller, not only aesthetically assess and remodel reality but at the same time embed it within a narrative. Take, for example, the photographs of every single car bombed during the Lebanese civil war between 1975 and 1990, collected by a certain Dr. Fakhouri, a historian. Such car bombs did indeed exist. Yet the archive created in this way undermined its authority: Is it all faked? In recent years, Raad has increasingly tended to name the fictitious character explicitly right from the start in order to replace the lost authority of historiography with the authority of narrative in the medium of art.

Anti-Archive: Gadji beri bimba!

When Walid Raad embeds real facts within fictional narratives, it is as if he were telling us: stop devouring documents and listen instead to the parable I am telling you by means of a few fragments extracted from them. Pitting the narrative against the archival in this way is actually quite surprising, given that contemporary art is, in large part, founded on two artistic acts from the first decade of the twentieth century, both of which were radically anti-narrative on the one hand, and potentially anti-archival on the other. They were Marcel Duchamp's invention of the Readymade and the definitive establishment of the sound poem as an artistic performance by Hugo Ball.

A sound poem can admittedly be written down and, as such, archived. But at the same time, Ball's recital in June 1916 at the Cabaret Voltaire in Zurich marked the birth of the idea of performance as a fleeting event associated with notions of the enigmatic and the refusal of disclosure – as, for example, in the much later *Dialogue Piece* (1969) by Lee Lozano in which she held conversations with all the artists she knew and noted briefly that they had taken place, yet without recording or transcribing the content.

Although there are photos of Ball's famous outfit with his tube-like bishop's miter, the sound poem itself is brought to life only at the moment of its intonation. Now, one might quibble that nothing is safe from the archive, that any and everything from music to intestinal rumblings to fantasies can be documented and archived. That may be true. But is it also art? The founders of Conceptualism and Dada were not exactly disposed to being all-too-willingly shoehorned into the epistemic framework. On March 1, 1916, just a few months before his remarkable performance, Hugo Ball noted in his diary, originally published in 1927 under the title *Flucht aus der Zeit* (Flight Out of Time): "Reality only begins at the point where things peter out."[5] Then, on June 18, he wrote: "We have now driven the plasticity of the word to the point where it can scarcely be equaled. We achieved this at the expense of the rational, logically constructed sentence, and also by abandoning documentary work . . ."[6] On June 23, he then noted that he had invented a new genre of poems.[7] For Ball, the archive was corrupted by its archivists; it had to be pushed ad absurdum in order to be alive.

The Über-Archival: One-Word Museums

The anti-archival and anti-narrative aspects of Duchamp and Ball form the necessary foundations on which artists such as Claes Oldenburg and Marcel Broodthaers were able to build their "museums." It was in 1965, in his New York loft, that Oldenburg began collecting found objects from the flood of cheap consumer products for his *Museum of Popular Art, N.Y.C.* – undersized chairs, oversized toothbrushes, plastic bananas, Mickey Mouse gloves, shop window decorations, imitation sweets, and so on – building up a critical mass of items whose novelty character or purely decorative function ranged from predominant to downright bizarre. Oldenburg first presented his *Mouse Museum* at documenta 5 in 1972 curated by Harald Szeemann; his *Ray Gun Wing* followed in 1977. The work chimed perfectly with Szeemann's extension of the concept of art into the wide field of popular everyday practice and into the narrow field of private obsession. The *Mouse Museum* exaggerated the museum-like tendency toward a ponderous solidification of the ephemeral: Oldenburg placed artifacts in a freestanding structure that had the outward appearance of a strangely formed cabinet of curiosities but which, from above, was recognizable as the famous silhouette of Mickey Mouse. Within the cabinet, the artifacts are aligned in diorama-like backlit showcases as though they were precious archaeological finds. This association adds a touch of irony to the cheap plastic kitsch. At the same time, the found objects do indeed take on the aura of the archaeological, especially with the patina of passing decades.

In *Musée de l'Art Moderne, Départment des Aigles* (1968–1972) by Marcel Broodthaers – also presented at documenta 5 in 1972 – there is a similar, perhaps even more heightened, sense of the mono-thematic oscillating somewhere between popular culture and archaeology. As in the case of Oldenburg, this is as much a parody as a serious appraisal of found cultural artifacts and, with that, as much a parody as a serious critique of the museum as institution. In Broodthaers's case, however, the emphasis is more on the latter. That is evident in the history of the work itself: the title was coined in 1968 as an ironic epithet for an event held in Broodthaers's own appartment, where there were not enough chairs available and so he simply borrowed some art transport crates. The title conjured up a fictional museum, underlining the absence of real institutional anchoring. The eagle stands for the enmeshment of art and power, kitsch and politics. It was not until 1972, at the Kunsthalle Düsseldorf, that the manifest presence of the eagle in advertising, propaganda, and trivial art was showcased, albeit without any scientific systematization based on chronological or content-related criteria. In the work of Oldenburg and Broodthaers, the anti-archival approach taken by the early pioneers of the Readymade and Dadaist poetry shifts toward the principle of a critical parody of the museum.

The Aesthetic of Administration: Files, Records, Shelves, Cupboards

The talk of the aesthetic of administration in regard to the Conceptual Art of the late 1960s and early 1970s became a sort of beacon of its reception.[8] From this perspective, the distilling of art into a statement using texts, files, or other commonplace forms of systematization and cataloging (in turn based on the reduced geometric forms of Minimal Art) almost inevitably could be read as an affinity to bureaucracy and economic control – to state power and capitalist consumption. Whether this took the form of photocopies of the artist's sketches and notes inserted into four binders, which were displayed, opened, on pedestals of equal size (Mel Bochner, *Working Drawings and Other Visible Things on Paper Not Necessarily Meant to Be Viewed as Art*, 1966), or work in the form of a quasi-scientific journal article about the mass culture of prefabricated architecture in US suburbs (Dan Graham, *Homes for America*, 1966), or even the eight filing cabinets presented on plinths by Art & Language at documenta 5 (*Index 01*, 1972), containing the compiled writings of the collective, together with an index in the form of a wall display – all of these works negated artistic authorship, the hand of the artist, "poetry" and so on, and not only through their methodical proximity to research, textual and archival work, but also in terms of formal aesthetics. The question that arises here is whether they mimicked the scientific positivism and administrative zeal of the Cold War in order to expose its contradictions and pitfalls – or whether they actually sought to be part of its triumph. It would be wrong to jump to the latter conclusion automatically, merely because of the lack of obvious parody as in the works of Oldenburg and Broodthaers. To do so would be to ignore the fact that, even though the forms themselves are redolent of the spheres of economic studies or tax returns, they are overwritten with idiosyncratic, decidedly anti-functionalist content. That in itself aims at the frustration of bourgeois observers' hopes of being distracted from the supposed object of their everyday working life.

I once picked up an anecdote: employees of the Deutsche Bank complained when works on paper by Hanne Darboven were to grace one of the floors of their Frankfurt headquarters. Their argument was that they had to study files and balances all day, so they didn't want to see the same thing on the walls. The added irony lies in the fact that Darboven herself, as co-heir of a Hamburg trading dynasty, had steered herself clear of that world by means of this particular artistic praxis. Just as Aby Warburg transformed the pact with his brother into a library, so too did Darboven transform her own trading background into art. Her stringent series of sheets of paper filled with longhand contrast with the collection of items ranging from bric-a-brac to collectors' pieces that she kept at her home in Rönneburg, on the outskirts of Hamburg, remaining unexhibited during her own lifetime. As Jan Verwoert writes:

> What stays behind, unexhibited, in the house, is a counterweight to what's displayed. . . . even though the house is filled to the rafters with thrift items, the objects are not arranged in any particular manner, they are simply stacked somehow and some seem almost untouched. . . . The collection is

> like a warehouse. What enters the depository can exit. None of the artefacts shows evidence of a desire to recuperate or incorporate them. Nothing is owned. Everything is stuff. Protected by walls of objects, Darboven is a hermit at an import-export office: she writes herself free from the symbolic weight of belongings.[9]

The work takes the form of an archive: index cards detailing the holdings of the depot. Yet there is no binding indicatory system for any connection between the outside (artistic praxis exhibited during her lifetime) and the inside (collection of items in her home and studio) – except in the person of the artist.

Body, Objects, Traces

On the face of things, parallels can be drawn between Hanne Darboven and Dieter Roth: Roth, too, demonstrates a striking contrast between strictly "administrative" works and installations brimming with things. However, Roth quite openly turns his own physicality – in all its energy and decay – into the very subject matter of this divided activity. Two of his key works are *Flacher Abfall* (Flat Waste, 1975–1976) and *Große Tischruine* (Large Table Ruin, 1974–1998). *Flacher Abfall* consists of more than six hundred standard binders in which, as the name suggests, almost every possible form of waste in his immediate surroundings has been filed away – from packaging to used toilet paper. An evidence room of waste. The parody of administrative bureaucracy is as evident here as the radical conservation of everything that has actually been discarded. *Große Tischruine* is its product-related counterpoint. Begun in 1974, the collection of materials on the studio table – cameras, brushes, tools, tape recorders, projectors – accumulated until it was exhibited for the first time in 1979 at Staatsgalerie Stuttgart. Further exhibitions featured an extension of this heap of material: if a projector had broken down, the new one would simply be attached to the old one. Hence: an anti-hierarchical omnium-gatherum and, at the same time, a charting of ongoing activity.

Following on from Roth, the principle of shortcircuiting production and waste can also be found in the work of Tomoko Takahashi, in whose installations things take on a life of their own, invading the very spaces from which they were once banned: as in her 1997 *Company Deal*, in which she flooded the office of a London marketing company with six weeks' worth of its own waste, from discarded binders to pizza boxes.[10]

In Stock

A larger complex takes the form of archival collections and appropriations of found photographs. Hans-Peter Feldmann, for instance, has been collecting, archiving, and presenting both his own photographs and found photographs since the late 1960s. His *Bilderhefte* (Picture Books, 1968–1974) not only include dedicated "art photography" but also possess something of the everyday. His observations reveal themselves clearly in the uncommentated arrangement and sorting according to easily-described motifs: mouths, female knees, airplanes. The hybrid realm of family album photos and incidental industrial photography as seen in magazines and newspapers spawns an intimate inventory of a life lived in the here and now.

Richard Prince takes a similar approach, initially, to the archive of stock photography: not his personal archive, but that of the Time Life publishing house. The advertising photographs became the material. *Untitled (three women looking in the same direction)* (1980) for instance features three rephotographed images aligned in the same format. Their seriality underpins the stereotype of the poses.

The appropriation of found images by artists – as in the case of Peter Piller – has freed the curatorial gaze to look at existing photographic archives previously ignored by the art world. Take, for example, the black-and-white photographs by Swiss police photographer Arnold Odermatt, who spent more than forty years photographing traffic accidents and other incidents with formal objectivity and in painstaking detail. By the same token, in the early years of the twenty-first century, curators such as Harald Szeemann, James Rondeau, and Urs Stahel presented Odermatt's work within an art world context.

#archive

"Interpol and Deutsche Bank, FBI and Scotland Yard, Inland Revenue and German Police, they all have our data at hand." These are the German lyrics, translated here, of the title song of Kraftwerk's 1981 album *Computerwelt* (Computer World). The archive is dumb; it has data. It is only through algorithmic connections that an image emerges, which, in turn, only becomes intelligent through interpretation. The Internet is the great meta-archive that enables dumbness and intelligent interpretation alike. Accordingly, we worry less today about the "poison cabinets" of the libraries than about the right to forget, hoping that not all the data pertaining to us personally will end up in the dragnet of state and private data collectors or be used against us in any way.

Against this backdrop, there is no need to point out just how strongly search engines and social media have changed the way we see images: phenomena such as memes, today's endlessly repeated visual jokes, are proof positive of this. In 2000, Boris Groys argued that the new was the result of negotiating the difference between the unimportant, worthless, profane, and that which is regarded as valuable enough to find its way into the archives (the library, the museum, etc.).[11] Although this distinction has not become invalid, it has nevertheless become enormously complex: we have to distinguish between the unimportant and the important with every Internet search we do. The preselection is not determined (as it is, ideally, in a museum) by means of scholarly evaluation, but by the criteria of earlier searches undertaken by ourselves and others. While that may normally have certain practical advantages (swarm intelligence), it can also result in ideological atrophy (swarm stupidity). So you have to take yourself and the machine by surprise. Oliver Laric, for instance, begins his work, which occupies the realm between the Web-based and the exhibition venue, by putting two seemingly incompatible terms, such as "Beckett and Teletubbies," into the search engine.[12] *Turbo Sculpture* (2011–2013) also sounds like just such a random combination of words. Aleksandra Domanović's work is a video slideshow composed of photos found on the Internet, documenting a strange phenomenon in the Balkan countries of former Yugoslavia: public statues of fictitious Hollywood characters in a region traumatized by civil war and still seeking a way of addressing its own recent history.

The porous and the profane – the garbage, the "unimportant" images and objects – have long since become the building blocks of the digital network. Without the keenly honed perceptiveness and knowledge of artists, who, for many decades now, have been mining the archives for new constellations, we cannot really hope to grasp the truths created on the Web.

1 Martin Mittelmeier, *Adorno in Neapel*, Siedler Verlag, Munich, 2013.

2 Walter Benjamin and Asja Lācis, "Naples," in: Marcus Bullock and Michael W. Jennings (eds.), *Walter Benjamin: Selected Writings*, trans. Rodney Livingstone et al., vol. 1, The Belknap Press of Harvard University Press, Cambridge, MA, and London, 1997, pp. 414–21, esp. p. 416. See also Mittelmeier, op. cit., p. 42.

3 Buchloh, however, reduces this issue to the question of whether Warburg was perhaps too optimistic in his view of photography's potential to reconstruct historical memory, whereas critics such as Kracauer and the constructivist avant-garde were, according to Buchloh, more likely to have been aware of the dangers of an untrammeled bourgeois dalliance with the flood of images. See Benjamin H. D. Buchloh, "Warburgs Paragon?: The End of Collage and Photomontage in Postwar Europe," trans. Pauline Cumbers,

in: Ingrid Schaffner and Matthias Winzen (eds.), *Deep Storage: Collecting, Storing, and Archiving in Art*, exhib. cat. P.S.1 Contemporary Art Center, New York, and Henry Art Gallery, Seattle, Prestel, Munich, 1998, pp. 50–60.

4 See Jacques Derrida, *Archive Fever: A Freudian Impression*, trans. Eric Prenowitz, University of Chicago Press, Chicago, 1997.

5 Hugo Ball, *Flight Out of Time: A Dada Diary*, ed. John Elderfield, trans. Ann Raimes, University of California Press, Berkeley, Los Angeles, and London, 1974, p. 53.

6 Ibid., p. 67.

7 Ibid., pp. 70ff.

8 See Benjamin H. D. Buchloh, "Conceptual Art 1962–1969: From the Aesthetic of Administration to the Critique of Institutions," in: *October*, vol. 55 (Winter 1990), pp. 105–43.

9 Jan Verwoert, "Chain-Smoking Clotho," in: *frieze d/e*, vol. 15, June–August 2014, available online at: frieze-magazin.de/archiv/features/klotho-raucht-kette/?lang=en, accessed 10/01/2014.

10 Rachel Withers, "Tomoko Takahashi," in: *frieze*, vol. 39, March–April 1998, available online at: www.frieze.com/issue/review/tomoko_takahashi/, accessed 10/01/2014.

11 See Boris Groys, *Under Suspicion: A Phenomenology of Media*, trans. Carsten Strathausen, Columbia University Press, New York and Chichester, 2012, p. 7.

12 See Pablo Larios, "Oliver Laric: Iconoclash," in: *frieze*, vol. 161, March 2014, available online at: www.frieze.com/issue/article/iconoclash/, accessed 09/01/2014.

A Riot on Every Page

Archive, Bureaucracy, Paranoia

Ben Kafka

Surely one of the greatest challenges facing any artist who wants to take on a bureaucracy – political, financial, educational, medical, or even cultural – is how dull the subject is. In fact, bureaucracies only seem to attract attention when they fail, and even such failures are so common as to be very nearly unremarkable. We are no longer surprised when a visit to the ministry, a letter to the university registrar, or a phone call to the bank ends in teeth-grinding, hair-pulling frustration. For the middle classes, indignation has become a way of life. For those who are more vulnerable, despondency has long since set in. These institutions, which are supposed to be the culmination of centuries of rationalization, seem to act every which way but rationally.

Fortunately, this has also made them an ideal subject for satire, and artists have eagerly risen to the task. Some of the greatest novelists of the modern era have concerned themselves with the absurdities of bureaucracy: Honoré de Balzac, Nikolay Gogol, Charles Dickens, Franz Kafka, José Saramago. So, too, some very good visual artists (Honoré Daumier, Saul Steinberg) and film makers (Terry Gilliam, Mike Judge). Even a few pieces of music (Erik Satie's "Sonatine Bureaucratique," Fugazi's "Waiting Room") have been composed on the theme.

But of course satire only takes us so far, and beginning in the last decades of the twentieth century artists started experimenting with a different sort of approach to bureaucracy. One of the first critics to take note of this trend was Hal Foster, who, in a justly influential essay published in the pages of *October* in 2004, identified "the archival impulse at work internationally in contemporary art."[1] Foster argued that while the impulse itself may not be new, there was nevertheless something new about the impulse. Instead of simply satirizing bureaucracy, artists were starting to behave like bureaucrats, fastidiously accumulating, arranging, cataloguing, and displaying texts, images, and objects.

Foster mainly focuses on multimedia artists, including Thomas Hirschhorn, Sam Durant, and Tacita Dean, but clearly the contribution of photography is crucial here. Thanks to the late Allan Sekula, we know how heavily bureaucracies have relied on photography. Only paperwork has been a more important medium (and perhaps also money, "the universal medium"). It was high time for photography to turn its lenses back at bureaucracy, not only through portraiture – as in the recent work of Jan Banning – but as evidentiary practice. My own model for such work is Hans Haacke's *Shapolsky et al. Manhattan Real Estate Holdings* (1971), with its assemblage of maps, diagrams, typescripts, and especially photographs that together present what Haacke called "a real-time social system as of May 1, 1971." *Shapolsky et al.* took on its considerable political, emotional, and aesthetic power by scrupulously documenting relations between the Shapolsky real-estate empire and various members of New York City's elite, including trustees of the Guggenheim, where the work was to be exhibited. I still remember the thrill when I first encountered this installation – it would have been the mid-1990s – a thrill that only increased when I learned of the censorship and purge it provoked. It is impossible to conceive of such archivally oriented photographers as Emily Jacir, Trevor Paglen, or Walid Raad – not to mention Peter Piller – without Haacke's contributions.

"To connect what cannot be connected," Hirschhorn tells Hans Ulrich Obrist in an interview cited by Foster. "This is exactly what my work as an artist is."[2] Foster sees in such work an attempt to impose an order on what is, to all appearances, an increasingly disordered world, though it seems equally true that, as in Haacke's case, the work can function to reveal the order behind a world that is only apparently disordered – but in fact quite tightly controlled. Turning to psychoanalysis, Foster wonders if we might detect in this archival impulse an attitude toward the world that could count as paranoid. "For Freud," he writes, "the paranoiac projects meaning onto a world ominously drained of the same (systematic philosophers, he liked to imply, are closet paranoiacs). Might archival art emerge out of a similar sense of a failure in cultural memory, of a default in productive traditions? For why else connect so feverishly if things did not appear so frightfully disconnected in the first place?"[3]

It's a provocative comment. Hal Foster is of course too subtle a critic to suggest that the artists themselves are paranoid. His point is that there is a certain style, a way of seeing, a way of making, that unites these artists. Crucially, for this art – if not the artists themselves – the issue is less about the reality of the connections than the fact of connectivity. That is to say, it does not matter whether the connections are real (as in Haacke's art) or fanciful (as in Piller's), as long as connections are being made. And here it seems worth introducing a distinction between "paranoid" archival art and what might be labeled its more "obsessional" counterpart. The latter would include work like Ed Ruscha's *Every Building on the Sunset Strip* (1966), which accumulates images in a quasi-archival manner but resists drawing any particular connections between them.

I would add that if there is in fact a paranoid sensibility to some archival art, it is not that of classic paranoia (paranoid schizophrenia), but of the lesser-known paranoia querulans ("querulous paranoia," also known as "litigious paranoia," "morbid querulousness," or sometimes "chronic grumbling"). The diagnosis, which is still in use, has its roots in the fin-de-siècle psychiatry of Richard von Krafft-Ebing and Emil Kraepelin, where it was used to describe individuals who found themselves locked in battles with authorities of one sort or another. These are the people who spend years of their lives drafting petitions, distributing leaflets, picketing offices, filing lawsuits, in an attempt to redress some grievance. Their kitchen tables overflow with letters, legal documents, lists of names; their bedrooms are packed high with boxes full of files. Like so many contemporary artists, these individuals settle on paperwork as a form of self-expression. They battle bureaucracy by behaving bureaucratically.

To be sure, this diagnosis is easily abused. Even Kraepelin, in his way, warned against mistaking the querulous paranoid from the person with a legitimate complaint. "Very perverse, quarrelsome, and also under some circumstances simply weak-minded people may bother the authorities in the same way as our patient," he explained. "To make the diagnosis of querulous delusion absolute, there must always be accurate proof that there really is a delusion to be dealt with."[4] Unfortunately, contemporary versions of the diagnosis have not been so careful. A few years back *The Guardian* published a piece about the revival of this diagnosis by British experts concerned about the number of complaints received by governments and corporations alike. Drawing on a study of "Unusually Persistent Complainants" published in *The British Journal of Psychiatry*, the newspaper offered a list of criteria, including "You pursue complaints for three years," "You sometimes turn up without appointments," "You will use three or more communication methods such as phone, fax, email or personal visits," and "You make emotive statements such as 'Should any reasonable person accept such treatment?'"[5] The question of the reality of the grievance had vanished entirely. With such criteria, anyone who complains about anything persistently enough – and emphatically enough – is at risk of being labeled paranoid.

Still, the potential for abusing this diagnosis – and psychiatric diagnosis more generally – should not distract us from its insights into a certain kind of aesthetic practice. Curiously, the authors of the article in *The British Journal of Psychiatry* even present aesthetic evidence to make their case for the continuity of the condition across the nineteenth and twentieth centuries. They describe how the "multiple underlinings, putting words in capital letters, and the liberal use of exclamation marks and inverted commas" found in the paperwork produced by their sample group had already been noted by Krafft-Ebing and Kraepelin in the late-nineteenth century (I can personally attest to its appearance in late-eighteenth-century archives as well). "Emphasizing words with multiple-colored highlighting pens is a modern variant, which we have also seen clinically among our querulant patients, some of whom produce a riot of color on every page of their voluminous complaints."[6]

There is something touching about this "riot of color" in the otherwise grimly grayscale world of bureaucracy. In fact, let it be Barthes' *punctum* in the studium of archival art. We are all far too cynical to see in this or any aesthetic gesture some sort of inherent revolt against power. But I would argue that there is, nevertheless, an element of resistance. The resistance implicit in this aesthetic gesture comes not from its commitment to fight against bureaucracy, but from its commitment to fight with it – which is also to say, to refuse to give up on it entirely. For even worse than the bureaucracy are the forces of neoliberalism and neonationalism that exploit our frustrations to further their agenda of weakening the welfare state. The frustrations of bureaucracy are still preferable to the depredations of capitalism.

I would like to thank Eric Banks and Thomas Y. Levin for helping me think through my contribution. It would be presumptuous of me to dedicate the essay to the memory of Allan Sekula, whom I only met once, but let it serve as some sort of small token of my admiration.

1 Hal Foster, "An Archival Impulse," in: *October*, vol. 110, Fall 2004, p. 3. For a rather different chronology of this archival impulse, see Sven Spieker, *The Big Bureaucracy: Art from Bureaucracy*, MIT Press, Cambridge, MA, 2008.
2 Hans Ulrich Obrist, *Interviews*, vol. 1, Charta, Milan, 2003, p. 322.
3 Foster, op. cit., p. 21.
4 Emil Kraepelin, *Lecture on Clinical Psychiatry*, rev. and ed. Thomas Johnstone, William Wood & Company, New York, 1904, p. 150.
5 "Mad, bad and paranoid – and persistent, too," in: *The Guardian*, November 12, 2005.
6 Grant Lester, Beth Wilson, Lynn Griffin, and Paul E. Mullen, "Unusually persistent complainants," in: *The British Journal of Psychiatry*, vol. 184, no. 4, April 2004, pp. 354–55.

Is the Human Brain an Archive?

Harald Welzer

> *"What you are telling us is a lot of inventions!" –*
> *"What I experience is a lot of inventions."*
> Max Frisch, *A Wilderness of Mirrors*

The human brain – or better put for our purposes: human memory – is not an archive, at least not in the sense that is usually ascribed to an archive. An archive, generally speaking, is a collection of information that, through some kind of storage medium – index cards, data, photographs, files, books, etc. – is collected and accessible. Publishers maintain archives, just as do newspapers and magazines, private individuals, and institutions of all sorts. In the archive-specific sense, "an archive is an institution that maintains archival materials or archival documents (synonym), and archival holdings must meet each of the following three criteria: a) they are created during the normal course of business by a legal or natural person; b) they are no longer needed for daily business; c) they have a lasting value."[1]

What is retained in human memory does not follow such criteria, nor is it limited to the storage of information or data. But surely the most important distinguishing factor is the fact that an ordinary archive, whatever type and function it might have, does not alter the information and data it holds. At the same time, a central feature of human memory is not just to *maintain* but instead to *modify* much of its contents through use. While archival material does not change when I use it, but is placed back in the same form that it had before, a retrieved memory is saved along with the situation in which it is retrieved and used. For example, if I recount a film scene and my conversation partner reacts to what I say, the social situation in which this memory is used will also be saved, thus becoming part of the memory. In a strict sense, one never uses the same memory twice, although, subjectively, it can certainly seem as though one always recalls the same, unchanging memory.

Each piece of content in autobiographical memory[2] thus has an internal as well as an external dimension – in other words, the contents of memories are not created autopoetically by the specific individual but are products of interactions with social and physical surroundings. Neuroscientific memory research refers to the internal neural activation patterns that belong to an idea or a memory as "engrams." Engrams represent the traces of all our experiences. Today less prominently discussed as important elements that comprise our memories are "exograms."[3] These include the people who came before us, traces of history, stories, objects, words, gestures – they are all extremely vivid and available traces of ideas and memories that can be activated, which we can and do access at any time. Exograms are any contents of external memory that can be used to respond to current needs and develop courses of action for the future. These can be written, oral, symbolic, objective, musical, habitual, and so on. In short, exograms can be any type of content that have either been developed as a means of human orientation (e.g., language) or can be used as such (such as the starry sky for navigating). To take a metaphor from quantum mechanics, such content leaps to exogram status in the moment it is recalled and used as external memory data.

In contrast to engrams, exograms are permanent, meaning that they transcend the temporal and spatial boundaries of individual existence and the horizon of personal experience. From an evolutionary point of view, the critical step in human phylogenetics was the development of symbols. As Merlin Donald has shown, this is because they enrich human cognitive potential to include an extremely powerful memory archive. "The biological memory records of the brain, known as engrams, differ from external symbols, or exograms, in most of their computational properties. Engrams are impermanent, small, hard to refine, impossible to display in awareness for any length of time, and difficult to locate and recall. . . . In contrast, external symbols give us stable, permanent, virtually unlimited memory records that are infinitely reformattable and more easily displayed to awareness. Moreover, exograms are much easier to search, and we can recall them with a variety of retrieval methods."[4] Human memory therefore has two representation systems at its disposal: an internal and an external. In this sense, any kind of archival content can take on the form of an exogram at any time, namely, when used by a person.

However, it cannot be assumed that exograms must always be accessed consciously, as is necessary when using an archive. Instead, the world in which one lives has a historical, cultural, and infrastructural texture. This can be understood as an exogrammatic structure that influences people's perceptions, interpretations, and decisions, without them being conscious of this influence. Neuroscientific memory research differentiates between autonoetic, meaning conscious memory data, and noetic, or implicit memory data. Similarly, sociocultural phenomena can also be attributed to implicit memory. For example, the "mnemic energy" of things already spoken of by Aby Warburg can only be grasped using scientific means with great difficulty and seems rather to belong to the field of aesthetic access. Thus, especially at the start of the last century, from Proust to Joyce and Musil to Nabokov, we find a wealth of research on the memory of spaces and things.

Despite the wealth of neuroscientific research on and theoretical advancements in recollection and memory, there is still a vacuum in the area of exogrammatic memory formation. What comprises memory and creates it every day – its texture – seems to be so complex and ephemeral that scientific instruments are bound to fail. On this side of scientific verification, we know that an individual memory first acquires form within social and cultural frameworks. Furthermore, that countless aspects of the reported recollections of others affect the interpretation and decisions of a listener directly and lastingly, that there are transgenerational transfers of experience that reach into the biochemistry of the neural processes in the next generations, and that the temporality of memory is not organized chronologically or linearly. This means that exogrammatic memory formation is ubiquitous and to a certain extent forms a universal archive, but one that cannot be systematized. Exogrammatic memory formation takes place through interactions, records, (moving) pictures, as well as spaces and landscapes. This is elucidated below.

Developmental psychology has produced impressive studies on how an autobiographical self that is able to look back on a distinct past is developed through the common practice of "memory talk."[5] During such *interactions*, it is also "learned" that references to the past are a constitutive part of living together in the first place, and that remembering is an omnipresent moment of actual social practice. This process is continued throughout one's life as a communicative updating of past experiences.[6] However, it is not necessary to speak explicitly about the past in order to form conversational memory. For example, when an anecdote is recounted at family gatherings, a kind of historical associative space is simultaneously communicated with regard to the circumstances, atmosphere, and habitus of the anecdotal figures. Such social interactions transport memory data casually and in passing, something that often goes unnoticed by those speaking.

The same may apply to *records* not even created for the purpose of later historical evaluation although they nevertheless form and format memories. Anything from an aphorism hanging in the kitchen to a bundle of love letters can find its way into the family archive. Ultimately, this includes all the documented utterances subsequently considered by historians to be sources. The archive only forms a special case of them.

As Gertrud Koch has explained, cultural products – plays, novels, and especially *images and films* – generally have an internal reference to the past, and they always convey historical constructs or readings of the past. Narrative and visual media always have at least one subtext, offering an interpretation of what has been seen to the recipient which might be entirely opposite to the commentary with which it is presented.[7]

But such media not only provide readings of the past; they also determine the perception of the present. Erving Goffman has noted that it is not only the sharing of experiences that follows such patterns and rules, but already the perception and interpretation of an event at the moment it occurs.[8] Cultural contexts are already effective in individual consciousness as structural matrices that process information. When importing "foreign" experiences into our own life story, we are dealing with a circular process. For example, when film scenes are used in the construction of "self-experienced" war stories, it may well be the case that they form a kind of collective sum of experiential fragments that have more or less been encountered by many former soldiers.[9] And there is no doubt that films base their narrative structure and other characteristics on preexisting narratives: the parole story of the simple soldier during the war, the narrative structure of the adventure, and the dramaturgy of the tragedy have all been adapted by the medium of film. Indeed, the entire relationship between narrative templates, experiences and their telling, and their depiction with the given visual material is inextricably complex.

Spaces are moreover also part of exogrammatic memory. Urban planning and architecture are ensembles in which historical times overlap in stone, concrete, and asphalt. Yet this form of memory construction – as demonstrated not only by historicism and the current trend of reconstructing castles – could also certainly be based on a politics of remembrance. Architects and urban developers are often motivated by the intention to accentuate a particular construct of a city's history. This is done by emphasizing certain historical relics and destroying others.

Regarding the interplay of engrammatic and exogrammatic modes of memory formation, I also feel it important to mention an early and little-known text by the later famous Gestalt psychologist Kurt Lewin. Drawing on his own experience, he demonstrated how experiences of landscape could seem completely different according to the specific mental and physical state of the person experiencing it. In 1917 Lewin used his experiences as an artilleryman as the basis for his phenomenology of the "war landscape." He describes his perception of the surroundings as dependent on the military movement of which the observer respectively finds himself. During an advance, the landscape appears to be "directed" and its characteristics such as woods, hills, and houses are defined according to their function in combat. However, during a retreat, the same landscape becomes an "undirected," peaceful landscape: "One perceives with astonishment that where there was only recently an emplacement, there is now land. The zone where one had to crouch and be on the defensive has become a part of the stretch of land that one must now traverse. Without having experienced an actual transformation, a field, meadow, or something similar has appeared instead of a place of battle and now only appears to have an agricultural relationship to the fields and woods around it. Instead of the directedness determined by the front, the fields and their margins now have different directions inherent in them."[10] It is here that the interdependence of engrams and exograms becomes aptly expressed: the context of individual experience determines how a person perceives, and thus recollects, this experience. The exogram defines the form of the engram.

All of this distinguishes the storage mode of autobiographical memory from that of the archive. However, in a more subtle sense, memory and archives have something in common: they are selective. Every affirmatively retained and retrievable memory stands in an invisible context to what, for whatever reason, was not preserved. Just as every archive has an inherent decision-making process that differentiates what can be an archival holding from what should be disposed of, the autobiographical memory likewise sorts what is, and what is not, preserved according to the degree of emotional significance.

In the case of human memory, this process of selection cannot be controlled or can be only controlled intentionally in marginal cases (which then leads to paradoxical results, for in order to intentionally forget something, one must remember what one wants to forget). Meanwhile, the archive is defined specifically by this underlying intention. This is also why what constitutes the human experience of time also cannot be found in conventional archives.

1 Martin Burkhardt, "2. Was ist ein Archiv?" in: *Gebrauchsanleitung für Archive*, available online at: www.historicum.net/no_cache/persistent/artikel/3062/, accessed 07/14/2014.

2 In neuroscientific memory research, a distinction is made between five memory systems: priming memory, procedural memory, and perceptual memory are unconscious forms of memory – and in part not even consciously accessible – and semantic and episodic memory as memory systems that are consciously accessible. Semantic memory includes knowledge independent of the context and time in which it was acquired, while the contents of episodic

memory entail a subjective index, meaning they are temporally and emotionally encoded. Starting at a developmental age of around three years old, episodic memory can be distinguished from more specific autobiographical memory, which does not have a systemic cerebral correlation but can be described as a bio-psycho-cultural functional system that maintains a sense of continuity and identity throughout one's life. See Hans Markowitsch and Harald Welzer, *Das autobiographische Gedächtnis: Hirnorganische Grundlagen und biosoziale Entwicklung,* Klett-Cotta, Stuttgart, 2005.

3 Merlin Donald, *A Mind So Rare: The Evolution of Human Consciousness*, Norton, New York, 2001.

4 Ibid., pp. 308–10.

5 Katherine Nelson, *Language in Cognitive Development: Emergence of the Mediated Mind*, Cambridge University Press, Cambridge, 1996.

6 David Middleton and Derek Edwards, "Conversational Remembering and Family Relationships: How Children Learn to Remember," in: *Journal of Social and Personal Relationships*, vol. 5, no. 1, February 1988, pp. 3–25.

7 Gertrud Koch, "Nachstellungen – Film und historischer Moment," in: Klaus E. Müller and Jörn Rüsen (eds.), *Historische Sinnbildung – Problemstellungen, Zeitkonzepte, Wahrnehmungshorizonte, Darstellungsstrategien*, Rowohlt, Reinbek, 1997, pp. 536–51, esp. pp. 537 and 547.

8 Erving Goffman, *Frame analysis: An essay on the organization of experience*, Harper and Row, London, 1974.

9 Harald Welzer, Sabine Moller, and Karoline Tschuggnall, *"Opa war kein Nazi": Nationalsozialismus und Holocaust im Familiengedächtnis*, Fischer, Frankfurt am Main, 2002.

10 Kurt Lewin, "Kriegslandschaft" (1917), in: Jörg Dünne and Stephan Günzel (eds.), *Raumtheorie: Grundlagentexte aus Philosophie und Kulturwissenschaften*, Suhrkamp, Frankfurt am Main, 2006, p. 322.

In Search of Lost Presence

Archival Fantasy in Memory of Frank Schirrmacher

Dietmar Dath

I am an unsteady, logically undetermined, yet nonetheless at least an intuitively sortable combination of archive and generator. In that respect I am like most people. Archive is everything I have been and have had. Generator is something that drives me to become and to want something other than what I am and have.

The Gallus district of Frankfurt am Main, where I live, is, in my view, a combination of archive and generator. But whereas I can at least distinguish between past (archive) and future (generator) when it comes to myself, the buildings of Frankfurt form the polar antiphony: from the window of my apartment, I can see the newspaper building where I work, and vice versa. But which of the two is the archive and which the generator is constantly changing, often at great speed: sometimes the book that is my current favorite will be lying next to the computer in the office, sometimes next to the bed in my apartment. As it happens, I tend to carry books around with me all the time: anthologies, magazines, newspapers, printed tonics, talismans. Indeed, when I worked for a few months at Suhrkamp publishing house, the night porter used to think, as she once admitted, that I was robbing the place and stealing valuable, rare old editions from their archives to sell on eBay, because she always saw me leaving the building with little stacks of books.

At the newspaper office, nobody thinks that; they see me there as someone who hauls just as much stuff from home to the editorial building as he does in the other direction.

The thing with the antiphony and the to-and-fro applies not only to physical material. There is also an alternation of informationally charged content between the mental spaces, be they here or there: sometimes I process my memories in the office and plan my future at home, and sometimes it's the other way round. What maintains the unsteady and logically undetermined connection between the archive and the generator in me is, of course, the kind of psychological presence we call the "self," in which René Descartes was so unhappily in love. By contrast, what links the archive and the generator in the street and architectural setting between Mainzer Landstrasse and Hellerhofstrasse is the kind of behaviorist presence that others call "Dietmar Dath," in whom, hopefully, somebody is in love – preferably not unhappily.

The archive needs the generator to ward off the cold (otherwise the data would freeze into dead crystalline gardens) or the heat (otherwise the data would melt and merge). The generator, on the other hand, needs the archive because something new can only be created out of something that already exists, and never out of nothingness (in accordance with the law of energy conservation).

The archive has a flirtatious attitude to the generator. It plays hard to get; it says that "you can't have me," that "you won't get what you want from me unless you are worthy of me," and other such patter to keep the generator at arm's length (though still within reach). The archive is mathematically literate; it knows that, as proof theory tells us, there are proofs of existence that are not constructive proofs – it is possible to demonstrate that this data or that data must exist, even though they are not available yet. The archive also knows that there is proof of existence that does not even indicate how much actually exists of the very thing whose existence they prove. For instance, it is possible to prove that there is a finite, rather than an infinite, number of solutions to a certain kind of equation, without necessarily being able to prove exactly how many solutions there are. The archive likes these little games because they unsettle the generator; the generator shouldn't get too cocky, otherwise it will start feeling superior to the archive and treat it as an inferior.

The generator's attitude to the archive, on the other hand, is impulsive and spontaneous. It likes to take little random samples at will from the archive's holdings. The generator, too, is mathematically literate and therefore knows that the unknown parameters within the abstract sampling area – the area of all possible occurrences of the observed values of a random variable or random vector – can be determined by means of the appropriate algorithms. The generator knows that the accuracy of predictions also depends on the sample size and its variables.

For instance, if I, as an unsteady and logically undetermined combination of archive and generator, want to know what's going on these days in the CD business, I take a look at the random pile of abandoned CDs that regularly builds up and disappears again on the glass table on the fourth floor of the editorial building on Hellerhofstrasse.

This glass table stands in the corridor right between my own office space and the office in which Frank Schirrmacher worked until mid-2014. He was my neighbor on that floor, separated from me by the corridor just as the editorial building itself is separated from my apartment building by the Mainzer Landstrasse.

On the glass table, then as now, there are not only CDs, discarded by music journalists, which are picked up and taken away by people from other departments, various staff members, and visitors. There are also books, placed there for our little community by the nonfiction editors and the literary editors.

Browsing through this little collection, taking random samples, deciding whether I want one of the CDs or books – these are evening activities: after 5 p.m., when the newspaper work is done, a little time is spent combing through e-mails and dealing with correspondence, and as a reward I sometimes go to the glass table to fish for a treat. But after a long day's work full of assimilating information and comparing data, I'm not always at my sharpest and so I often make the same mistake: I set down the book, or books, that I am carrying on the glass table while I look through the pile to see if there's anything worth taking, and once I've found something, in my absent-mindedness and exhaustion, I end up leaving my own stuff there.

If I'm lucky, I notice my mistake while I'm still in the building – after all, I often return to my office after I've chosen my treat. But if not, I have to hurry to get my stuff back before somebody else finds it and thinks it's there for the taking.

I once lost a little pile of essays by Carl Schmitt that way – those slim, green paperbacks published by Duncker & Humblot. They must have been from around the turn of the last century, the "zero years" that don't correspond directly with the ten years between 2000 and 2010, but somehow, in terms of historical perception, equate to the time between September 11, 2001, and the inauguration of Barack Obama as President of the United States on January 20, 2009.

When the Schmitt essays went missing, I was so scatterbrained that I didn't even notice until several days later. It wasn't hard to reconstruct what had happened, though, as I'd made the same mistake a few times before. In search of the lost books, I went from office to office, trying to figure out which of my colleagues might be interested in Carl Schmitt.

Nobody had seen the books, and nobody had the slightest clue.

It is said of criminals who haven't yet been caught that they return time and again, almost obsessively, to the scene of the crime. It is as though the connection between archive and generator had been disrupted in those who remember having done something that nobody but themselves should know, and which therefore nobody can confirm, and so it seems that they seek to repair that connection by attempting to reconstruct their spatial orientation in this way.

What applies to criminals, it seems, also applies to scatterbrains: although I had seen (and therefore knew full well) that the lost books were no longer lying on the glass table, I kept returning there for days after each failed attempt to find them elsewhere. It probably wasn't actually the books I was really looking for – I was examining the moment and the place of loss, in a bid to correct both somehow and to create a new relationship between memory and the option of action, between archive and generator.

And so I kept coming back to the glass table, kneeling down beside it, bending over it, examining the books that were lying there: perhaps those Carl Schmitt paperbacks would turn up after all, perhaps somebody might have put them back, perhaps my books had changed color and format. One evening, as I was going about this idiotic task, I was spotted by Frau Ruppel, the strict and longstanding secretary of editor Schirrmacher, who knew all the newspaper's secrets.

"What are you up to there?" asked Frau Ruppel in her typically straightforward tone. I told her and, shaking her head, she replied, "Well, I'll have a look." And she disappeared into her boss's office. Within five minutes she had returned with the Schmitt books in hand. I straightened up, thanked her and said, rather stupidly, "But what if he comes by my office now and sees and thinks I've stolen them from him? After all, he must think they belong to him now because they were on the table for anyone to take." "So what," said Frau Ruppel, "You're just a poor subeditor; you need them more than he does. He can buy the books himself."

I am sitting here, writing. Frau Ruppel has retired. Frank Schirrmacher is dead.

People we have been accustomed to having around, and who we then rarely see or not at all, are not easily archived. They play a part in the way our own generator continues to function.

I leaf through the coffee-table book *Zeitung* (Newspaper) from the *Peter Piller Archive*: lots of pictures, few captions. Everything is there; but it is not clear what the things that are there really are.

Which in itself could be read as a visually figurative concretion of the truth of mathematical proofs of existence – something exists, but that is all I know about it.

That can be comforting.

Certainty is definitive. In a sense, it kills. Uncertainty is a call for appropriation, for the formulation of use values.

The future is what we call the time in which all the archives will have, themselves, become generators – and vice versa.

This Is Not an Archive
Internet as Temporary Storage

Geert Lovink

Here is our challenge: understanding the multiple meanings of "sharing is caring" as it unfolds according to our architectures.
Johan Sjerpstra

The Internet is not an archive. It serves the purpose of what Wolfgang Ernst calls "temporary storage."[1] Despite a range of popular myths, scholarly references, and journalistic presumptions, there is no evidence that computer networks should be considered "archives." Due to state and corporate interests, the "network of networks" is simply too dynamic and too unstable to be considered useful for the long-term preservation of cultural artifacts. When bills go unpaid, sysadmins move on, retire, or decease, operating system versions are not upgraded, companies go bankrupt, and telco policies change, then hard disks crash, connectivity breaks down or simply shuts off, server racks are forgotten, disconnected, and then sold off for scrap and recycled, and domain names expire or are not renewed. It is this dynamic vitality of the Internet that runs counter to the implied stasis of the archive.

If the idea of the "archive" is too formal, too institutional, maybe we should rather talk of the Internet as an instant pseudo-archive of the present? As a meta "anarchive" (Siegfried Zielinski) it can be seen as an "alternative activity to the archive,"[2] a market anarchy based in military origins and specifications, filled with incomplete indexes, dead, or corrupted links of half-finished digitization projects, or outdated information in forgotten databases. In short, an open collection of collections and half-baked or forgotten assemblages filled with "wild archaeologies" (Knut Ebeling), driven by the "logic of multiplicity and a wealth of variety," and that do not "pursue a fixed design." The contrast Zielinski paints between institutional archives in which "things are collected, selected, preserved, restored, sorted from the perspective of an (apparatus-related) whole" and the "autarkic, resistant, easily perishable, autonomous anarchive" may be a false one.[3] The previous contrasting condition of state-run institutions and large corporations operating against alternative subcultures – a condition that originated in the

1960s – has been superseded altogether by a different data monster of a third kind, a creature dominated by contradictory and conflicting entities; the minoritarian monopolies, extra-legal security agencies, and the flattering narcissism of mono-dimensional social media interactively consumed by the self-obsessed masses.

From the earliest days of their inception, computers have been good at one very specific thing: number crunching. This is what they start doing from the moment they are switched on. There is no such thing (yet) as an idle computer. Only after being switched off can it rest and be silent. Computers lack the primal capacity to be passive. They are manic machines. From the late 1960s the Internet has been perceived as a medium of lively electronic exchanges, connected machines that communicate, just for the sake of it, with or without the human presence of the admin aka user. Be it through streaming data or the transfer of fixed files, what happens in a network is communication between nodes. The Internet consists of endless cycles of servers contacting other servers, copying this, storing that, time and again.

Fifty years after its inception, the "vitalist" aspect of the Internet is only understood by network administrators, and the general knowledge about the built-in back-and-forth has gradually been pushed to the background. How many ordinary users are still using Unix commands such as telnet, ping, and traceroute? Only the machines themselves, or specialized users like sysadmins, do. The techno-vitalism of the Internet is one of the main obstacles to perceiving the Internet as an archive. If only we could let devices "sleep" and wake them up remotely in order to restore the connectivity . . . without versioning problems. Inadequate or broken backwards compatibility is a plague of the computer age – and future generations will despise us for it. This is not simply a user interface or a computer language problem. Those can all be learned. It's the jumbled mass of incompatible and disused data formats, file extensions, and network protocols that make the "archive" inaccessible and impossible.

Taken off the network, a server is merely a collection of digital data, not much more than a storage device. As we all know, the storage capacity of computers continues to grow exponentially, and the cost per byte is going down at the same rate. The problem we're fighting with here is the static world view of a computer terminal (smartphone, tablet, notebook, etc.) that requests access to a database elsewhere in order to transfer requested files. With archives it usually doesn't work like that. Traditionally, archives were (and still often are) protected against instant access. Bureaucratic, and often economic, rituals pre- and proscribed who had access to what data. This was even the case with public records. The cool rationality of instantaneous access to any possible data is a utopia of a frictionless, automated rationality that fully understands, and incorporates, the need to store all information and make it universally accessible.

The archive with its claim of *longue durée*, on the other hand, has to be protected against the present. It is a conspiracy against time. Digitization has made "time capsule" procedures a thing of the past and shifted the work to an endless ritual of neo-medieval copying (and upgrading) of the digital material, endlessly translating it from substrate to substrate, from file format to file format, in order to prevent hackers from deleting the material, to compensate for hardware that is prone to failure, and files from becoming unreadable through the demise of formats and standards.

Needless to say, analogue paper archives of the past did not have an eternal life either. All objects, digital or not, dissolve into entropy. Thus, a primary concern and purpose of an archive is to safeguard a given set of materials until the world is ready to process it. In some case this can be months or a few years, in others a century or even more.

Therefore, the future of the archive remains resolutely offline. Online material is the exception. Digitization and "open access" are the demands of a civic democratization movement and the culturally specific procedures of (Western) network societies. This is how neoliberal late-capitalist society reproduces its legitimacy. Even future assemblages of computer hardware, software, and connectivity will be far too fragile and unstable to last very long untouched. The dependency on the undisrupted flow of electricity alone makes computer networks profoundly unreliable, which explains why so many digital companies locate themselves near uninterruptible power supplies, like hydroelectric dams in the case of Google, or geothermal power in the case of IBM.

Computer networks can only thrive with the massive 24/7 attention paid by millions of users, workers, and volunteers who maintain the vital elements and systems of its existence. This is the true rationality of techno-vitality. The Internet cannot be stashed away and re-accessed a few decades or centuries later. It only exists as a dynamic entity whose sustainable operation depends on the permanent involvement of a multitude of highly trained players: server software programmers, network managers and analysts, sysadmins, local and global telcos, and fiber-optics companies (and their shareholders), satellite programs, as well as national regulatory and global governance organizations such as the Internet Assigned Numbers Authority (IANA), Internet Corporation for Assigned Names and Numbers (ICANN), and Internet Engineering Task Force (IETF).

A special place in the current delicate Internet ecology is taken by the rapidly growing number of large-size data centers. At first glance their remoteness and futuristic techno-look suggest that these data storage locations are here to stay –

and could even be considered the Internet archives we are looking for. But nothing could be further from the truth. Sudden and simple changes in geopolitics, electricity pricing, land and real-estate costs (and, not to forget, the rapid aging of the used electronics), and the profitability of rentable rack space can all cause an overnight closure of such facilities. Services can be banned by national policies, hosting companies can go bankrupt, and the taste of the online multitudes for apps and content can suddenly shift.

All archives require curation. This is why there are, strictly speaking, no Big Data archives. These unsorted, raw data collections can – and will be – stored for the next generations to investigate them. However, it remains an open question as to whether or not thousands of servers holding Big Data will hold any cultural value, much less if anyone will have a look at them. Google's AI project, under the guidance of mad scientist and member of the US corporate royalty Ray Kurzweil, is presently digitizing and storing edited, curated, and reviewed material, guided by the Google mantra "let others do the work first that we won't pay for." This condensed, high-value information is the kind of heritage you want to feed your AI. Simple machines will do the slavery work of working with Big Data. The same could be said of attempts to archive the Internet. The best parts of Brewster Kahle's Internet Archive[4] are the curated parts. The random website part and Wayback Machine are plagued by technical issues, such as outdated plug-ins or missing pages.

A similar problem exists in the context of search engines. At a certain point adding extra information flips the entire set of online assemblages of data into entropy. This might also be the reason why the "deep web" remains hidden and why we should be happy to "merely" access 30 percent of the Net. Should all Facebook updates and tweets become fully searchable? Must the data generated by common household appliances and remotely controlled by mobile apps be fully searchable? The multimillion results on ordinary search terms no longer bothers us. While we've become inured and complacent to the malignant growth in data and the resources it requires, perhaps it should concern us.

One of the more precise proposals in this direction is Henry Warwick's PhD dissertation, written in 2012 for the European Graduate School (Saas-Fee, Switzerland). In June 2014, a summary of this study appeared, entitled "Radical Tactics of the Offline Library." Here, Warwick reflects on the rise of "personal portable libraries." Because of the dramatic drop in prices of consumer data storage devices, we can now store 10 000 books on a USB flash drive purchased for 30 CHF, and we can pass around 120 CHF hard drives containing 800 feature films. Entire university libraries can fit onto a 3 terabyte drive. Because of draconian copyright regimes that were devised prior to and as a reaction against the ubiquity provided by the digital realm, the online world has become a precarious trap. Henry Warwick concludes:

> Resisting the precarities of the online and the encroachments of the security state, in a reversalism of older practices based in the replication of knowledge substrates, the Personal Portable Library propels us into a future beyond the sociopathic greed of Proprietarian regimes. Owning and managing a Personal Portable Library is more than just good research practice – it's a *radical tactic* of resistance against informational feudalism, a strategy of dismantling Proprietarian theory, and an ennobling act of sharing the fruits of culture with all, for the good of all.[5]

The term library may be preferable after all to the over-theorized notion of the archive, which, until recently, was primarily associated with the file-controlling (nation-)state. In a time where storage size (now measured in terabytes) and access no longer matter, all that users care about is the social setting. Soon, indexed digital libraries attached to offline Wi-Fi networks or meshnets will be social centers where members consult for their informational needs, combined with the irresistible plus of humans meeting other humans through reading clubs, orgnets, meet-ups, LAN parties, cafés, student lounges, and other hybrid forums. When multiple lifetimes worth of media, books, and information can be easily stored and shared on cheap consumer technology, how will the politics and poetics of our digital libraries play out when we design the next generation of public libraries?

Thanks to Henry Warwick for his comments and his never-ending streams of ideas.

1 "The immediateness of the retrieval of immense volumes of data through online databases contends with an increasingly maximum usability period, which contemporary culture knowingly accepts," Wolfgang Ernst, "Temporary Storage," in: Claudia Giannetti (ed.), *AnArchive(s)*, Edith-Russ-Haus für Medienkunst, Oldenburg and Walther König, Cologne, 2014, p. 176.

2 A deliberate provocation from my side, in friendly dialogue with German media theorist Siegfried Zielinski, in: Giannetti, op. cit., p. 23.

3 Siegfried Zielinski, in: Giannetti, op. cit., p. 23.

4 See https://archive.org/, accessed 09/02/2014.

5 Henry Warwick, *Radical Tactics of the Offline Library*, Institute of Network Cultures, Amsterdam, 2014, p. 49.

Authors' Biographies

Elisabetta Antonelli (b. 1976) studied German and Romance Languages at the universities of Zurich and Florence before training as a journalist at the MAZ media school in Lucerne, Switzerland. Today, she is head of the pool of reporters for *Landbote*, the daily newspaper serving Winterthur and environs, now in its 178th year. Antonelli lives in Winterthur.

Joerg Bader (b. 1955) has been working as an art critic and curator since the 1990s. In 2001 he took up his post as director of the Centre de la photographie Genève, where he has curated exhibitions such as *La revanche de l'archive photographique* (2010) and *fALSEfAKES* (2013). Since 2002 he has also been teaching at the Haute École d'Art (HEART) in Perpignan. Bader lives and works in Geneva and Belo Horizonte.

Dietmar Dath (b. 1970) is a writer and translator. A former editor-in-chief of *Spex* magazine, he was an editor for the arts and culture section of the German daily *Frankfurter Allgemeine Zeitung* from 2001 to 2007 and has been their in-house film critic since September 2011. Dath has published novels, nonfiction books, and essays on science, aesthetics, and politics, including the novel *The Abolition of Species* (Seagull Books, 2013) and the polemical pamphlet *Maschinenwinter* (Suhrkamp, 2008). Dath lives in Freiburg im Breisgau and Frankfurt am Main.

Jörg Heiser (b. 1968) is co-editor of *frieze*, co-publisher of *frieze d/e*, and is an art critic writing, amongst others, for the *Frankfurter Allgemeine Zeitung*. He is a visiting professor at Kunstuniversität Linz, Austria, and teaches at the Hochschule für Bildende Künste Hamburg. *All of a Sudden: Things that Matter in Contemporary Art* (Sternberg Press) was published in 2008, and his next book *Double Lives: Art and Pop Music* will also be published by Sternberg in 2015. Heiser lives in Berlin.

Ben Kafka (b. 1976) is a historian and psychoanalyst. He teaches critical theory and cultural history in the Department of Media, Culture, and Communication at New York University. His book *The Demon of Writing: Powers and Failures of Paperwork* was published by Zone Books in 2012.

Max Küng (b. 1969) is a reporter and columnist for *Das Magazin*, the weekly round-up of the Swiss publisher Tamedia-Verlag. He has published three books of his collected works with Edition Patrick Frey, among them *Pensive Racing Drivers* (2013). His first novel is due for publication by Rowohlt in 2015. Küng lives in Zurich.

Geert Lovink (b. 1959) is a media theorist, Internet critic, and author. He has been a researcher since 2004 in the School for Communication and Media Design at Amsterdam University of Applied Sciences (HvA), where he is also founding director of the Institute of Network Cultures. His publications include *Zero Comments* (Routledge, 2007) and *Networks Without a Cause: A Critique of Social Media* (Polity, 2012).

Maren Lübbke-Tidow (b. 1968) is an author, critic, and curator. From 1998 to 2011 she was editor, and from 2011 to 2014 editor-in-chief, of *Camera Austria International* (Graz/Berlin). She has curated numerous group exhibitions on behalf of Camera Austria (Graz), as well as solo exhibitions by such artists as Wolfgang Tillmans (2007), Annette Kelm (2008), and Michael Schmidt (2012). She is currently preparing solo exhibitions by Erik van der Weijde (2014) and Sven Johne (2015). Lübbke-Tidow lives in Berlin.

Peter Piller (b. 1968) studied at the University of Fine Arts (HFBK) in Hamburg. Since 2006 he has held a professorship at the HGB Academy of Visual Arts in Leipzig. His ten-volume artist's book series *Peter Piller Archive* and several further artist's books have been issued by Revolver Publishing. Major solo exhibitions include shows at the Museum für Gegenwartskunst Siegen (2003), Witte de With Center for Contemporary Art, Rotterdam (2005–2006), Kunsthaus Glarus (2007), Kunstmuseum Bonn (2009), and Kunstverein Braunschweig (2011). Piller lives and works in Hamburg.

Dieter Roelstraete (b. 1972) is the Manilow Senior Curator at the Museum of Contemporary Art Chicago. His many publications on contemporary art and culture can be found in exhibition catalogues, journals, and magazines such as *Artforum*, *e-flux journal*, *frieze*, *Mousse Magazine*, and *Texte zur Kunst*. He is a member of the team headed by Adam Szymczyk, curator of documenta 14, which will be held in Athens and Kassel in 2017.

Thomas Seelig (b. 1964) has been curator and keeper of the collection at Fotomuseum Winterthur since 2003 and, since 2013, its co-director with Duncan Forbes. As curator, he has been responsible for exhibitions such as *Research and Invention: Investigations with Images in Contemporary Photography* (2007), *Karaoke: Photographic Quotes* (2009), *Status: 24 Contemporary Documents* (2012), and *Concrete: Photography and Architecture* (2013). Seelig lives in Winterthur.

Ludwig Seyfarth (b. 1960) studied art history, literature, and philosophy in Hamburg and now works as a freelance author and exhibition curator. He has been visiting professor and lecturer at several German art schools and has curated exhibitions for venues such as Kunsthaus Hamburg, Villa Merkel in Esslingen, and, on a regular basis since 2010, for KAI 10 | Arthena Foundation, Düsseldorf. Seyfarth lives in Berlin.

Marcus Steinweg (b. 1971) is a philosopher. He teaches philosophy at the Braunschweig University of Art (HBK). He is editor of the journal *Inaesthetics* (Merve) and curator and author of *Kunst und Philosophie / Art and Philosophy* (published by Verlag der Buchhandlung Walther König, 2012). He has also collaborated on many projects with the Swiss artist Thomas Hirschhorn. Steinweg lives in Berlin.

Harald Welzer (b. 1958) is a sociologist. He is director of the nonprofit organization Futurzwei, which he co-founded. Since July 2012 he has been honorary professor of transformation design at the Europa University in Flensburg. His many publications include *Climate Wars: What People Will Be Killed For in the 21st Century* (Polity, 2012) and *Soldaten: On Fighting, Killing, and Dying; The Secret WWII Transcripts of German POWs* (with Sönke Neitzel, Alfred A. Knopf, 2012).

Bibliography

2014

Archiv Peter Piller: Materialien (F). Nachkriegsordnung
Ed. Éditions Centre de la photographie Genève
Nieves, Zurich, 2014
20.5 x 15.5 cm, 76 pages, 36 illustrations
Softcover
Book accompanying the exhibition *Belegkontrolle*,
Centre de la photographie Genève, December 13, 2014 – February 22, 2015

Archiv Peter Piller: Materialien (E). Peripheriewanderung Winterthur
Ed. Fotomuseum Winterthur
Nieves, Zurich, 2014
20.5 x 15.5 cm, 68 pages, 32 illustrations
Softcover
Book accompanying the exhibition *Peripheriewanderung Winterthur*,
Fotomuseum Winterthur, December 13, 2014 – February 22, 2015

Archiv Peter Piller: Umschläge
Dashwood Books, New York, 2014
17 x 24 cm, 52 pages, 30 illustrations
Softcover

2011

Archiv Peter Piller: Kraft
Ed. Christoph Keller
JRP|Ringier, Zurich, 2011
15 x 10.5 cm, 132 pages, 60 illustrations
Hardcover
Book accompanying the exhibition *Archiv Peter Piller: Kraft*,
Kunstverein Braunschweig, June 25 – August 28, 2011

Archiv Peter Piller: Schlaf
Ed. Barbara Wien
29.5 x 40 cm, 80 pages, 38 illustrations
Hardcover
Book accompanying the exhibition *Archiv Peter Piller: Am liebsten sitze ich allein im Auto*, Galerie Wien Lukatsch, Berlin, February 18–April 15, 2011

2010
Archiv Peter Piller: Materialien (D). Peripheriewanderung Graz
Edition Camera Austria, Graz, 2010
20.5 x 15.5 cm, 128 images, 62 illustrations
Softcover

Archiv Peter Piller: Materialien (C). A40 Bochum Dükerweg
Ed. Christoph Keller
Nieves, Zurich, 2010
20.5 x 15.5 cm, 62 pages, 48 illustrations
Softcover

2009
Peter Piller: Siedlung
Kodoji Press, Baden, 2009
24 x 17 cm, 20 pages, 10 illustrations
Softcover

2008
Archiv Peter Piller: Deko + Munition
Ed. Galerie Michael Wiesehöfer, Cologne
Nieves, Zurich, 2008
42 postcards
14.8 x 10.5 cm
Softcover

2007

Peter Piller: nimmt Schaden
JRP|Ringier, Zurich, 2007
14 x 17.5 cm, 128 pages, 122 illustrations
Hardcover
Book accompanying the exhibition *nimmt Schaden*,
Kunstforum Baloise, Basel, June 11 – November 16, 2007

Archiv Peter Piller: Zeitung
Ed. Christoph Keller
JRP|Ringier, Zurich, 2007
27.6 x 29 cm, 384 pages, 1'618 illustrations
Hardcover
Book accompanying the exhibitions *In Löcher Blicken*,
Salzburger Kunstverein, Salzburg, February 15 – April 15, 2007;
Ungeklärte Fälle, Hamburger Kunsthalle, Hamburg, May 13, 2007 – April 6, 2008;
Ästhetik und Langeweile, Kunsthaus Glarus, September 9 – November 18, 2007

Archiv Peter Piller: Materialien (B). Peripheriewanderung Bonn
Eds. Beethovenstiftung, Bonn, and Christoph Keller
Revolver Verlag, Frankfurt am Main, 2007
20.5 x 15.5 cm, 123 pages, 86 illustrations
Softcover

Peter Piller: Teilzeitkraft
JRP|Ringier, Zurich, 2007
17 x 12 cm, 160 pages, 79 illustrations
Softcover

Peter Piller: Nijverdal/Hellendoorn
JRP|Ringier, Zurich, 2007
21 x 16 cm, 90 pages, 86 illustrations
Hardcover

2006

Archiv Peter Piller, Vol. 10: Bedeutungsflächen (da ist es)
Ed. Christoph Keller
Revolver Verlag, Frankfurt am Main, 2006
20.5 x 15.5 cm, 96 pages, 90 illustrations
Softcover

Archiv Peter Piller, Vol. 9: (Pfeil)
Ed. Christoph Keller
Revolver Verlag, Frankfurt am Main, 2006
20.5 x 15.5 cm, 96 pages, 90 illustrations
Softcover

2005

Archiv Peter Piller: Materialien (A). Dauerhaftigkeit / Duurzaamheid
Eds. Witte de With and Christoph Keller
Revolver Verlag, Frankfurt am Main, 2005
20.5 x 15.5 cm, 32 pages, 28 illustrations
Softcover
Book accompanying the exhibition *Peter Piller Archives*,
Witte de With, Rotterdam, November 19, 2005 – January 8, 2006

Archiv Peter Piller
Griffelkunst, Hamburg, 2005
10.5 x 14.8 cm or 14.8 x 10.5 cm (format individual postcards)
7 folders with postcards each containing 10 to 16 postcards
in a cardboard folder

2004

Archiv Peter Piller: Von Erde schöner
Ed. Christoph Keller
Revolver Verlag, Frankfurt am Main, 2004
28 x 28 cm, 320 pages, 310 illustrations
Hardcover

Peter Piller: Vorzüge der Absichtslosigkeit
Ed. Christoph Keller
Revolver Verlag, Frankfurt am Main, 2004
29.6 x 21.4 cm, 216 pages, 200 illustrations
Softcover
Book accompanying the exhibition *Vorzüge der Absichtslosigkeit*,
Museum für Gegenwartskunst, Siegen, October 14, 2004 – January 30, 2005

Archiv Peter Piller: Unangenehme Nachbarn
Revolver Verlag, Frankfurt am Main, 2004
15 x 9.5 cm, 28 postcards in a cardboard folder

Archiv Peter Piller, Vol. 8: Auto berühren
Ed. Christoph Keller
Revolver Verlag, Frankfurt am Main, 2004
20.5 x 15.5 cm, 96 pages, 88 illustrations
Softcover

Archiv Peter Piller, Vol. 7: Regionales Leuchten
Ed. Christoph Keller
Revolver Verlag, Frankfurt am Main, 2004
20.5 x 15.5 cm, 96 pages, 102 illustrations
Softcover

2003
Peter Piller: gültig?
Ed. Christoph Keller
Revolver Verlag, Frankfurt am Main, 2003
20.5 x 15.5 cm, 28 pages, 72 illustrations
Softcover
Book accompanying the exhibition *gültig?*, Bonner Kunstverein,
February 12 – March 23, 2003

Archiv Peter Piller, Vol. 6: Stein des Anstoßes
Ed. Christoph Keller
Revolver Verlag, Frankfurt am Main, 2003
20.5 x 15.5 cm, 96 pages, 90 illustrations
Softcover

2002

Archiv Peter Piller, Vol. 5: Schmuckstück/Schandfleck
Ed. Christoph Keller
Revolver Verlag, Frankfurt am Main, 2002
20.5 x 15.5 cm, 96 pages, 90 illustrations
Softcover

Archiv Peter Piller, Vol. 4: Die Verantwortlichen sind einstimmig
Ed. Christoph Keller
Revolver Verlag, Frankfurt am Main, 2002
20.5 x 15.5 cm, 96 pages, 90 illustrations
Softcover

Archiv Peter Piller, Vol. 3: Noch ist nichts zu sehen
Ed. Christoph Keller
Revolver Verlag, Frankfurt am Main, 2002
20.5 x 15.5 cm, 112 pages, 106 illustrations
Softcover

Archiv Peter Piller, Vol. 2: Diese Unbekannten
Ed. Christoph Keller
Revolver Verlag, Frankfurt am Main, 2002
20.5 x 15.5 cm, 96 pages, 90 illustrations
Softcover

Archiv Peter Piller, Vol. 1: Durchsucht und versiegelt
Ed. Christoph Keller
Revolver Verlag, Frankfurt am Main, 2002
20.5 x 15.5 cm, 112 pages, 106 illustrations
Softcover

2001

Peter Piller: 3 Hefte

Regionales Leuchten, Auto berühren, Überschattete Aufnahmen
Wiens Verlag, Berlin, 2001
21 x 14.8 cm each; *Auto berühren*: 16 pages, 16 illustrations;
Regionales Leuchten, Überschattete Aufnahmen: 12 pages, 12 illustrations
Softcover

2000

Miej serce i patrzaj w serce! / Mein Herz und ansehen im Herzen!

Ed. Hans Andree
Materialverlag, Hamburg, 2000, from the series *Zum Buch 3*
21 x 12.5 cm, 20 pages
Softcover

1998

Peter Piller: Noch ist nichts zu sehen

Materialverlag, Hamburg, 1998
21.5 x 23.1 cm, 112 pages, 53 illustrations
Softcover

1997

Peter Piller: speiseeiswagen im wendehammer

Ed. Jutta Hercher
Materialverlag, Hamburg, 1997
24 x 21 cm, 110 pages, 40 illustrations
Softcover

This catalogue is published on the occasion of the exhibition
Peter Piller: *Belegkontrolle* (Document Control) at Fotomuseum Winterthur,
December 13, 2014 – February 22, 2015.

The exhibition takes place simultaneously in Winterthur and at
the Centre de la photographie Genève. Additional exhibition partners
are the Städtische Galerie Nordhorn, March 14 – May 17, 2015,
and the Kunsthalle Nürnberg, June 13 – August 16, 2015.

Editor: Thomas Seelig
Design: Iza Hren, Christoph Keller
Copy-Editing: Dawn Michelle D'Atri, Daniela Janser, Amy Klement
Translations: Ishbel Flett (essays by D. Dath, J. Heiser, M. Küng, P. Piller and T. Seelig),
Alisa Kotmair (essays by E. Antonelli, J. Bader, H. Welzer),
Laura Schleussner (essays by L. Seyfarth, M. Lübbke-Tidow), and
Paul Feigelfeld (essay by M. Steinweg)
Production: Printmanagement Plitt, Oberhausen

Published by
Verlag der Buchhandlung Walther König, Köln
Ehrenstr. 4, D-50672 Köln

Bibliographic information published by the Deutsche Nationalbibliothek
The Deutsche Nationalbibliothek lists this publication in the Deutsche Nationalbibliografie;
detailed bibliographic data are available in the Internet at http://dnb.d-nb.de.

Printed in Germany

Distribution:
Germany & Europe
Buchhandlung Walther König, Köln
Tel. +49 (0) 221 / 20 59 6-53, Fax +49 (0) 221 / 20 59 6-60
verlag@buchhandlung-walther-koenig.de

UK & Eire
Cornerhouse Publications
70 Oxford Street, GB-Manchester M1 5NH
Fon +44 (0) 161 200 15 03, Fax +44 (0) 161 200 15 04
publications@cornerhouse.org

Outside Europe
D.A.P. / Distributed Art Publishers, Inc.
155 6th Avenue, 2nd Floor, USA-New York, NY 10013
Fon +1 (0) 212 627 1999, Fax +1 (0) 212 627 9484
eleshowitz@dapinc.com

ISBN 978-3-86335-673-6